CAVIAR

By Susan R. Friedland

CAVIAR

RIBS

CAVIAR

Susan R. Friedland

CHARLES SCRIBNER'S SONS
New York

For my mother,
and the memory of my father

Library of Congress Cataloging-in-Publication Data
Friedland, Susan R.
Caviar.
1. Caviar.   I. Title.
TX385.F75   1986   641.6'92   86-11901
ISBN 0-684-18437-0

Published simultaneously in Canada by Collier Macmillan Canada, Inc.
Composition by Maryland Linotype; Baltimore, Maryland
Manufactured by Fairfield Graphics; Fairfield, Pennsylvania
Designed by Ruth Kolbert

First Edition

Acknowledgments

Many people were generous with their time, information, and recipes. I am grateful to Dan Halpern, Lydie Marshall, Ann Schube, and Paula Wolfert for allowing me to use their recipes. Pat Bear and Naomi Bernstein of For Your Information, Inc., were enormously helpful and generous. The research material they provided was invaluable in terms of content and time saved. For sharing their vast knowledge and their time, I'm indebted to the caviar pros, Christian Petrossian, John Roberts, and Gerald M. Stein. I'm thankful also to family and friends who offered information, encouragement, enthusiasm, and who good-naturedly ate five-course meals, each course of which included caviar.

Contents

᪻

"If it were not a pleasure, it would be an imperative duty to eat
caviare. . . . It is said that when sturgeon are in season, no less
than two-thirds of the female consists of roe. It is certainly odd
to think of a fish weighing perhaps 1,000 pounds being two-thirds
made up of eggs. . . . At such a rate of reproduction, the world
would soon become the abode of sturgeons alone, were it not
the roe is exceedingly good."

E. S. DALLAS
Kettner's Book of the Table (1877)

INTRODUCTION

More than any other food, caviar conjures up wealth and status, luxury and celebration; it is full of legend and magic. Caviar is the universal symbol of both privilege and decadence. Christian Petrossian, whose father and uncle introduced Russian caviar to Paris in the 1920s, says about Caspian sturgeon caviar: "It is more than a food, it is a dream."

Caviar ("black pearls"), along with saffron ("the spice with the price of gold") and truffles ("black diamonds"), is the most expensive food in the world. Saffron is more expensive, but a pinch goes a long way and no one gobbles it with a spoon; you *can* have enough saffron. Truffle satiation is usually reached after one or two or a dozen shavings. Caviar alone of the three would be sought, consumed, and addictive even if it were inexpensive.

The source of all the drama, poetry, and sometimes even intrigue is the processed roe of the Caspian female sturgeon. In France and in the United States, there are laws specifying that only the processed roe of the sturgeon may be called caviar. In France, the laws are as strictly enforced as the *Appellation d'Origine Contrôlée* regulations for wine. In the United States the approach is more relaxed: as long as the fish is named on the jar or package, the word *caviar* can be used to describe any processed fish eggs. And the roes of many fish are prepared like caviar: salmon, whitefish, flying fish, cod, crab, steelhead trout, sea urchin, herring, lumpfish, carp, paddlefish, hackleback. The results are sparkling and often delicious beads of various tastes, colors, sizes, and textures. These roes are plentiful and inexpensive; many of them are produced in the United States and have begun to appear with great regularity and reliability in shops and on restaurant menus. They combine well with other foods to create elegant, tasty, and beautiful dishes to serve as hor d'oeuvres, soups, appetizers, entrées, and salads.

Snob appeal should have no place in the perfect enjoyment of caviar. Even the most expensive sturgeon caviar from the Caspian Sea should be appreciated for what it is—a food of great subtlety and textural interest. The more affordable caviars from salmon and other fish offer much the same textural interest as well as a wide variety of tastes and far more uses in combination with other foods. The best of the Caspian should be eaten with just a spoon (and what kind of spoon is a matter of amusing controversy), or perhaps on buttered toast or blinis. You can, of course, splurge and combine it with pasta or baked potato: many such combinations can be superb. But these same foods are also delicious and satisfying with salmon caviar, American sturgeon caviar, golden whitefish caviar, or any of the fresh or pasteurized processed roes.

Caviar, for all its rarefied reputation, has existed as a delicacy almost as long as Western civilization. Salted and pickled sturgeon eggs were known in Greece in the eighth century B.C. Aristotle wrote of caviar in the fourth century B.C. During the Roman Empire, caviar was brought to the table to a chorus of trumpets and flutes and placed in the midst of garlands and flowers.

In the twelfth century, Henry II of England placed the sturgeon under royal protection. Sturgeon was known as the "royal fish"; when caught it had to be handed over to the kitchen of the feudal lord. Edward II, who ruled England in the early fourteenth century, wrote an edict referring specifically to sturgeon fishing.

In the sixteenth century, sturgeon was so plentiful in the estuary of the Rhône that it was the cheapest fish in southern France. Rabelais, the sixteenth-century French physician, satirist, and humorist, wrote of "caviat" in *Pantagruel*. By 1520, when Pope Julius II praised it, sturgeon had become a favorite of European royalty and aristocracy. In *Hamlet* (Act II), Shakespeare used the caviar metaphor to mean above the taste or appreciation of the masses, something too good for the general population: "The play, I remember, pleased not the million; 'twas caviare to the general."

Until the end of the nineteenth century, sturgeon was common in European and American waters. It was still caught in the Seine and Hudson rivers in 1900. The rivers entering the Atlantic and Pacific oceans, the southern part of the North Sea, the Baltic, the Black Sea, the Sea of Azov, and the Caspian Sea were all rich in sturgeon. The only surviving eastern Atlantic populations are based in the rivers Gironde in France and Guadalquivir in Spain, and at Lake Ladoga in the Soviet Union. The sturgeon fishery in the Gironde estuary was of some importance. Caviar processing was organized there in the seventeenth century by Louis XIV's efficient minister, Jean Baptiste Colbert. It was abandoned and then reorganized in great secrecy after the First World War by Monsieur Prunier, of the Paris fish restaurant, who had spent a holiday in the area. Perceiving a neglected opportunity, he sent a knowledgeable Russian émigré to the region; caviar was produced there for years. This lightly salted caviar didn't travel much beyond France, but it did account for a significant proportion of the caviar consumed in that country.

Until the end of the last century, about 250,000 pounds of sturgeon roe were produced in North America each year, about 100,000 pounds of it in Penns Grove, New Jersey, on the Delaware River. And a good portion of that was exported to Europe, mainly Germany. In *A Report on the Sturgeon Fishery of Delaware River and Bay*, published in 1899, John N. Cobb recalled, "The earliest settlers to this country were especially struck at the immense numbers of the sturgeon seen in the Delaware, and their letters to the home fold in England and Germany contain frequent references testifying to their wonderment."

William Penn himself made a special note of the fish. By the end of the nineteenth century, the catch had declined but the fishery itself was still quite elaborate. Legislation had been passed to prevent other fishermen from catching or harming young sturgeon (known as *mammoses*). Over 1,000 men were employed in the sturgeon fisheries in Delaware and Pennsylvania. The fishing itself was done by gill net.

Sturgeon were also found in large quantities in the Hudson River, where the pink flesh of the fish, which resembles veal in taste, was sold as "Albany beef," and the salted roe was given away with a nickel glass of beer, much as peanuts are today and for much the same reason: the salt made the drinker thirsty and so he ordered more beer.

Unfortunately, the waters were overfished; industrialization and the unregulated discharge of its wastes caused pollution deadly to sturgeon and most other fish; dams were built; and for most of the twentieth century, sturgeon have almost completely disappeared from all but the Caspian Sea, the Black Sea, and the Gironde River. There is hope, however, that by the end of this century, large quantities of healthy sturgeon will reappear in the Hudson and other American rivers.

There are only two classes of fish: those with a bony skeleton and those with cartilaginous "bones." The sturgeon has a skeleton that is bony only in part, and some authorities have placed it in a special subclass of bony fish.

From fossilized remains we know the sturgeon that swim around today are remarkably similar to the sturgeon of 100 million years ago. Their backbone is cartilaginous; but they have rows of bony scutes along their bodies, and the head is covered with hard bony plates. The head also has a snout under which are four barbels that look like whiskers. Toothless and unprepossessing, the sturgeon burrows with the snout and feels with the barbels to find its food on the sea or river bottom. It eats worms, plant life, crayfish, insect larvae, and mollusks. Carp, another bottom-feeder, is often consumed by the much larger *huso* or beluga sturgeon. Man is the sturgeon's only predator. Linnaeus, the eighteenth-century Swedish naturalist, classified the species: *Acipenser* of the family Acipenseridae. The vernacular, sturgeon, has its root in the German name Stör. It is probably derived from the verb *störer*, to root, which is how the sturgeon seeks its food.

Although there are many species within the genus, only three or four are universally acknowledged as producing the best caviar: beluga, ostera, sevruga, and sterlet. These three or four populate the Black and Caspian seas and Sea of Azov, which supply the costliest, rarest, and most exciting caviar. The beluga, probably the most famous, is also the largest. It grows to 14 or 15 feet long, and can weigh up to 2,000 pounds, though 800 or 900 pounds is average. Its eggs are the largest: 2½ to 3 millimeters in diameter. Its color ranges from light steel gray to dark gray. It takes twenty years for the female beluga to mature and yield its eggs, which accounts in part for the rarity and high cost of beluga caviar.

Osetra sturgeon weigh between 250 and 600 pounds, and grow to about six feet. The female starts to produce eggs at ages twelve to fifteen. The brownish gray eggs have a golden tint and a strong fruity flavor.

The sevruga, with its distinctive long pointed snout in the shape of a scythe, is the smallest, about 50 pounds and the most abundant of the sturgeons. It matures in seven years. Its eggs, dark gray to black, are the smallest, but the flavor is strong. The sterlet, virtually extinct, was the smallest species of sturgeon and was once considered the finest for eating. The "golden caviar" of the czars was considered by many to be the ultimate delicacy. It comes from albino sturgeon of any of the species. In Stalin's time, the Soviet leader received two-fifths of all the golden caviar fished, the shah of Iran received two-fifths, and the remaining one-fifth went to the chairman of the Russo-Persian fisheries company, a coveted job. Each of the mature species yields 10 to 20 percent of its body weight in roe.

The roe does not become caviar until it has been processed; unprocessed roe is extremely bland. First, of course, the fish must be caught. In the Caspian Sea, an elongated 163,500-square-mile salt lake between southeastern Europe and Asia, which is the largest inland body of water in the world, there are two catches annually, in the spring and in the fall, each lasting four months. The fishermen string nets across the rivers that lead to the sea. The fish are caught in the estuary regions on their journey from salt to freshwater in the spawning seasons. The quality of the river bottom will affect the taste of the fish and the caviar—a muddy bottom will impart an unpleasant, earthy taste. In the Caspian, old wooden boats, equipped with ancient engines and net winches, are manned by experienced fishermen, usually the sons and grandsons of men who fished the same waters. Once or twice a day, the fishermen inspect the catch in the nets, hoping that amid the wide variety of fish caught in them will be a female sturgeon.

The males are valued, as are the females, as a food fish: pickled, smoked, or fresh, sturgeon provides fine eating. Vesiga, the spinal marrow of the sturgeon, is a gelatinous substance, aspiclike when cooked, and a classic ingredient for coulibiac, a many-layered fish and pastry creation that has been called celestial—manna for the culinary gods. In addition, isinglass, a very pure form of gelatin prepared from sturgeons' air bladders, is commercially valuable. It is used chiefly as a clarifying agent in making jellies and glue. Isinglass was formerly used to make thin transparent sheets; in "The Surrey with the Fringe on Top," from the musical *Oklahoma*, it provided the material for the "curtains you can pull right down, in case there's a change in the weather."

The live female sturgeon is brought immediately to one of the processing centers where thirteen complicated and speedy operations are conducted in less than fifteen minutes to get the precious and valuable roe. The first of these steps is a sharp blow to the head with a wooden mallet—no easy job, when you consider a 600-pound monster slithering around, intent on escape. In a stainless-steel room that looks like and maintains the same standards as an operating room, the fish is weighed before the roe is removed. The fish must be dressed live because the egg membranes in dead fish deteriorate so quickly that they rupture. Each fish is given a number that will identify it until the caviar is sold to its ultimate consumer. Immediately after she is stunned, a long incision is made in the belly of the comatose female sturgeon. The worker removes the roe sacs and places them on a giant sieve whose openings are slightly larger than the size of the eggs in the sacs. Slowly the sacs are manipulated over the grating and the eggs are caught in a stainless-steel bucket below. The eggs are washed in fresh water and gently drained. It is then that the master taster takes over.

A member of the elite brotherhood that includes master winemakers and perfumers, the taster will grade and determine the future of the roe. It is not an exaggeration to call roe grading an art. The uniformity and consistency of the grain, the size, color, fragrance, and flavor, the gleam, firmness, and the vulnerability of the roe skin are all factors that must be considered, and an accurate judgment made within minutes. There are caviar lovers who swear they can tell the identity of the master by rolling a bit of caviar around their tongue. Maybe they can. For beluga, the master sorts the eggs and determines their grade according to size and color (o, oo, ooo, the last is the largest and considered the best; color is graded A or nothing). The bigger and lighter eggs are rarer and thus become the more expensive caviar.

The next step is deciding how much salt to use in the preservation. This step is utterly crucial because the salt not only preserves the roe but ripens it into caviar. The master's judgment is critical because it determines how much the finished caviar will be worth both commercially and gastronomically.

Malossol, meaning "little salt" in Russian, is the most prized. The eggs must be top quality, young enough, and of uniform color and size to accept the malossol treatment, which means using less than 5 percent salt in relation to the amount of roe receiving it. (There are no U.S. laws governing and policing this and some so-called malossol is *very* salty.) The master has a trained eye for evaluating color and size, a trained nose for smell, a trained touch for firmness (much of his work is done with his fingertips), and most important, an educated palate for discerning flavor.

A determination must be made and sorting done in only two or three minutes because the quality of the roe changes rapidly. The weather and the product's destination also play a part in the amount of salt used. Caviar destined for the United States and Germany can be processed with salt and only salt—4 to 6 pounds per each 100 pounds of eggs to be considered malossol. Borax in combination with salt can be used for caviar going to France and other parts of Europe and the Middle East. Caviar processed with borax has a sweeter taste and less shrinkage than that treated with salt only. Caviar prepared with borax requires only 2 or 3 percent salt and results in moister caviar. That is, the more salt used, the more liquid is drawn off; therefore the caviar is drier and will more quickly lose its firmness. In the 1940s, a few baby bottles washed in borax were found to have a poisonous residue (large amounts *are* toxic), and its use has been outlawed in this country since. FDA inspectors will immediately return an entire shipment if they discover even trace elements of borax.

The kind of salt used is the next variable in the process. Before 1941, salt from the salt deposits in the Astrakhan Steppe was used almost exclusively. When chlorine was introduced to purify the water, that salt could no longer be used. Nowadays a chemically purified salt is used for the preparation of caviar. The salt is blended by hand and it forms a light brine with the moisture in the roe. The small amount of fat present in the roe is drawn off by the salt. The roe is then placed on fine sieves and these are shaken until the caviar is dry. The caviar is then immediately transferred to two-kilo (4.4-pound) tins. Larger tins would put too much weight on the eggs on the bottom, which would make them burst. The lids of the tins are varnished so as not to impart a metallic taste to the caviar. They have concave interiors so that when pressure is applied, any remaining brine will be forced out. The identifying number of the fish and the grade given the roe by the master are affixed to the tin, which is secured with a large rubber band to create an airtight seal. The rubber bands also allow flexibility: the eggs will settle during the journey and to compress them too tightly would ruin them. This has proved to be the most reliable packing system: the lid is always pressed firmly on the caviar, and if the tin is filled properly to start with, no air can get in to ruin the contents. The top layer is called the mirror, and as soon as the tin is opened for repackaging for the consumer, it will reveal the state of the entire 4.4 pounds.

So-called barrel caviar is prepared in the same way as the malossol. The difference is the amount of salt used. With malossol, less than 6 percent of the weight of the eggs is salt; between 6 and 10 percent salt is used in the barrel caviar. Early in the spring catch, March or the first weeks of April, the roe of all sturgeon remain firm and resistant, and with few exceptions, most is suitable for malossol. At the end of April and into May, when the temperature increases, the roe loses its firmness and is usually processed as barrel or pressed caviar.

Pressed caviar (*payusnaya* in Russian) is made from more mature eggs, usually caught later in the fishing season, as well as from eggs broken in the processing, or eggs too ripe to be preserved whole. The cleaned, salted eggs are put into a large linen or cheesecloth sack. The sacks are put in a machine much like a cotton baler or winepress and subjected to intense pressure. About 20 percent of the fatty liquid is pressed from the sack and the result is a marmaladelike substance. It takes five pounds of fresh eggs to make one pound of pressed caviar, and the resulting intense flavor is highly valued, indeed, even revered, by connoisseurs. It is packed and shipped in the same two-kilo tins used for the fresh whole-grain caviar.

Malossol caviar, pasteurized in Russia as well as in other countries, is very important economically to the trade because, if stored under proper conditions, it will keep for at least a year. The caviar, packed in one-, two-, and four-ounce jars, is hermetically sealed under vacuum and "cooked" at 149 degrees Fahrenheit. Taste, consistency, but mostly texture suffer from this processing, pasteurized caviar is, however, less expensive than fresh and it can still be delicious to eat.

Great care and attention are paid to the packing and shipping of the fresh tinned caviar. To insulate against warmth, three-foot-high barrels are lined with reeds. A square structure is built into them in which there is room for six layers of tins, each layer containing nine tins and each tin containing 4.4 pounds of caviar. So there will be no movement during transport, every three tins are firmly sewn into a linen bag. Each cask contains eighteen bags, fifty-four tins. All the hollow spaces are filled with finely ground ice; then a circular mat, cut to the measure of the top of the barrel, is put on top and the cask is closed with the lid. The lid is marked with the number originally assigned to it by the master, the gross and net weights, and the quality of the caviar. The bottom of the cask is drilled two to four times to allow the melting ice to drain off. Caviar that will make the journey entirely in refrigerated containers is packed in two-kilo tins, twelve to a case with each group of three placed in a sack-cloth sleeve. No ice, no draining—much simpler. The caviar is forwarded from the fisheries scattered all along the Caspian Sea to Astrakhan, at the mouth of the Volga River. From there the casks are shipped by steamer and refrigerated railway cars to Leningrad, where they are examined for quality by a state commissioner before the caviar is licensed for export. All containers are then sealed with lead. Barrel caviar is exported from the Soviet Union in oak or linden barrels weighing from 110 to 120 pounds.

What makes this caviar so expensive? So good? So coveted? The Caspian caviar sets the standard by which all others are judged: it has a subtle saline flavor, without tasting fishy; the "berries" (as they are known in the trade because ideally they should resemble ripe huckleberries) should be whole, firm, and well oiled. The size of the grain is a matter of preference, not quality. So for that matter is the color of the grain. The glutton may claim to delight in the largest grain and lightest color, but the color of the roe changes with the natural pigmentation of the fish and the time of year the fish was caught. When the beluga is near spawning, her eggs are most mature and lightest in color; when she is furthest from spawning, the eggs are black. The commercial order of desirability is not always the caviar lover's order. In the Caspian area itself, many sturgeon fishermen and caviar processors prefer osetra to beluga on grounds of taste; some like sevruga best, feeling that the other caviars are too subtle in flavor. In fact, it is often the relatively inexpensive pressed caviar that is preferred. The "best" caviar is what *you* like best.

The high cost is attributable to the scarcity of sturgeon; the many years it takes the female sturgeon to produce eggs; the difficulty of catching, processing, and transporting the caviar; and the need for continuous refrigeration and monitoring because the roe is so perishable (as little as one hour at room temperature will ruin fresh caviar). The Caspian Sea, in which the Russians strictly limit the season for fishing, has been shrinking. They are trying to redirect the flow of rivers to compensate for this loss of water but it is a very long-term project. There are indications that the sea was 250 feet higher than it is today and that it was connected to other seas. Even in the last thirty years, the level has dropped by more than eight feet. More water is being lost by evaporation than is being added by rivers. Today Astrakhan is over 137 miles from the harbor. In 1902, it was twenty-four miles closer to the harbor. Soviet scientists fear that although the damming of the Volga for hydroelectricity and irrigation projects will regulate the flow of the river and prevent floods, it will at the same time increase the water area of the Volga and thereby aggravate the loss of water in the Caspian. The irrigation canals drawn off the Caspian will further reduce its levels. Most alarming, the percentage of salt will be correspondingly increased. It is the salinity and the temperature of the water that most significantly affect the conditions in which the sturgeon thrive.

Iran, which has 440 miles of Caspian coastline, was a great processor and exporter of caviar until the overthrow of the shah in the late 1970s. That country used to produce about 180 to 200 tons of caviar a year, 30 to 40 of which were exported to the United States. (That figure may be misleading because some people claim the Russians bought a good deal of Iranian caviar and exported it under their own label.) Religious Iranian Muslims never ate it themselves because, as a product from a nonscaly fish, it is prohibited to them (as it is to strictly observant Jews). The Iranians exported virtually all their caviar, in contrast to the Russians who consume a great deal of their own supply themselves. In fact, Russians consume more than any other nationality. The Iranian caviar was first-rate, equal to top-quality Russian, and in some cases better. After a period of uncertain reliability and supply, Iranian caviar is reestablishing its competitive quality. Given world political conditions, it is impossible to predict the future.

The overthrow of the shah, and the closing of that source of caviar, came at a time when the American sturgeon population was increasing, and Russian and Iranian techniques for processing the roe became known here through contacts with Russian and Iranian émigrés.

Since the early 1970s, domestic caviar has experienced a remarkable renaissance. The campaigns of the last few years to clean up American rivers, together with conservation and antipollution measures, have increased the sturgeon population. Atlantic, white Pacific, and Lake sturgeon, as well as several freshwater species, are native to the United States but hard to identify since American producers of caviar don't print species names on their labels. The field is populated with large and small producers along both coasts as well as in the Mississippi-Missouri River system. No one wants to talk about sources, because it is often against state law to purchase any part of the fish, including the roe, but they encompass north and south Atlantic waters, the Pacific, the Great Lakes, Alaska, and inland rivers including the Arkansas in Oklahoma, the Osage in Missouri, and the Columbia in Washington and Oregon, as well as sources in the Midwest and deep South.

In the South and Midwest, the fishermen are after the long-billed sturgeon known locally as "shovelnose cats" or paddlefish. They are usually about six feet or longer, and weigh anywhere from 75 to 150 pounds. The processing of the eggs is similar to that of Russian caviar: the eggs are extracted, washed, and then pressed by hand through a rectangular stainless-steel mesh with ¼-inch holes. Next, the eggs are blended by hand with noniodized salt (about ¾ ounce for each pound of eggs). After blending, the eggs are poured into a fine-mesh sieve and allowed to drain for ten to fifteen minutes, until they are somewhat drier—not dry, but not soupy. The caviar is then packed in three-and-a-half-gallon drums and stored in refrigerated rooms at a temperature of 26 to 28 degrees Fahrenheit (the high salt content prevents freezing at that temperature) for anywhere between one week and three months. It is then transferred to another refrigerated room with a temperature of about 38 degrees Fahrenheit to be packed into seven- or fourteen-ounce tins, ready for distribution to the retailer.

The so-called white sturgeon, *Acipenser transmontanus*, is actually gray in color. It is found primarily in the Columbia River in Oregon and Washington, though it also plies the waters of the Ghehalis River and Willapa Bay in Washington and the Fraser River in British Columbia. Slightly smaller than the Caspian beluga, it is the largest of the seven species found in the United States and shares Northwest waters with its smaller cousin, the green sturgeon (*A. mediostris*), whose skin is actually olive green with scattered deep red-and-white markings that resemble snowflakes.

Fish and game laws in California prohibit the selling of the sturgeon or its eggs. Fishermen may catch them, as they do the green sturgeon in the Sacramento River, for personal consumption; the legal limit is an optimistic one per day per fisherman. The eggs are prized and the demand has evolved into a black-gold rush. The black market California roe brings good money to the sturgeon fisherman, at least ten dollars a pound, and one good-sized female can hold thirty or forty pounds. Not surprisingly, people involved in this network of sturgeon poaching, selling, and caviar production are reluctant to talk about it, and the California Department of Fish and Game has a difficult time enforcing the laws because the fishermen *are* allowed to catch the fish. There are no such laws in Oregon and at least one California processor buys his eggs from fishermen who catch the sturgeon in the Columbia River.

In California, Missouri and the Soviet Union, experiments are under way to farm sturgeon. In the Soviet Union, the goal of one program, called Natural Controlled Breeding, is to preserve the species. In California, a former supervisor of Soviet acquaculture is developing methods for removing the sturgeon's eggs by Caesarean section. The fish are anesthetized and their roe removed. They are then returned to the water to live on and produce again. The mature eggs can be extracted in two-year cycles, allowing every other year for unhindered reproduction. Techniques are also being developed to breed sturgeon in vast ponds, like those used in the South to grow the plebian catfish. The Soviets have been experimenting with breeding techniques so that sturgeon that may take fifteen years to mature can be brought to maturity in only six years. The Soviet system uses genetic selection (the Soviets have attempted crossbreeding with the American species, which are characteristically strong and adaptable with their Caspian Sea varieties), artificial feeding, and temperature regulation. The Soviets have not been forthcoming with their results.

The American sturgeon caviar industry is still in its infancy, but it has enormous potential. American caviar is less than half the price of Caspian beluga, and much more than half as good. For those who like their food to be politically pure, American caviar has neither the taint of an Iranian religious fanatic, nor of the Russians, whose sins are daily reported to us.

The Chinese are also entering the international caviar market. Produced from sturgeon caught in the Amur and other rivers in Manchuria near the Russian border, the caviar is marketed in this country under the name Keluga. The *huso Dauricus*, a close cousin of the Caspian species, is huge: some reportedly grow to 2,000 pounds and can yield up to 400 pounds of roe. The Chinese have been producing some caviar for domestic consumption for years, but those who have tasted it there claim it was mushy, oversalted, and gelatinous. A California couple skilled in caviar making were invited by the Chinese to inspect and improve the Chinese caviar production. They spent several months directing the processing operations for foreign shipments. The result is excellent: a medium-grain, black, moist, nonoily, lightly salted caviar. Not much is produced (about 5,000 pounds a year) and the price is competitive with Russian caviar.

·   ·   ·

Though it is only the processed roe of the sturgeon that can legally be called caviar, many other roes are processed the same way. The most widely available and affordable nonsturgeon caviars in this country are the roes of salmon, whitefish, lumpfish, and cod. Each is different in size, texture, and taste; all are available fresh or pasteurized. (In all cases, the fresh is better than the pasteurized. You will have to search for fresh lumpfish caviar, but it's worth it.)

Salmon used to be plentiful in almost all the rivers of western Europe and North America. In past centuries it was a common and inexpensive food fish—so common, in fact, that indentured servants in Colonial America stipulated that they could not be fed salmon more than once a week. Farm workers in Brittany resigned themselves to eating it three times a week and servants in Norway, five times a week. The record seems to have been held by the monks of the French Abbey of Lavoute-Chillac: they were patient until they began to find salmon on their plates more than once a day; when they rebelled so violently, the prior hastily promised "to restore calm, that thereafter they would eat salmon only once a day and not more than three days a week." Dickens wrote that salmon and poverty went together, so we may assume that in the nineteenth century it was still a very inexpensive fish.

The first fish specifically mentioned in American history is the salmon. Eric the Red, in the tenth century, reported that the Vikings encountered "larger salmon than they had ever seen before." Frederick Marryat, after visiting the United States in 1837, told his English compatriots: "Their salmon is not equal to ours." Nevertheless, New England salmon was still good enough to create a local tradition. Longfellow described John Endicott as

> a solid man of Boston.
> A comfortable man, with dividends,
> And the first salmon, and the first green peas.

In the Northwest, salmon was the principal food of the Northwest Indians. Few societies have been so closely wedded to a single food as the Indians of that area were to salmon. Three-quarters of their food was fish and shellfish, and three-quarters of that three-quarters was salmon. In several Indian languages the word for "salmon" was also the word for "fish."

In their expedition, which started in 1804, Lewis and Clark reported on the amazing abundance of salmon in the Columbia River, still one of the greatest salmon rivers in the world. The explorers reached it shortly after spawning season and had to force their boats through thick swarms of floating salmon that had spawned and died. William Clark wrote in his journal: "The number of dead salmon on the Shores and floating in the river is incredible to see and at this season [the Indians] have only to collect the fish, split them open and dry them on their scaffolds."

The red roe of the salmon was spread on the rocks to dry and then smeared on bread like butter. Some Indians put the roe in bags made from deer stomachs and hung the bags in their smokehouses. They kneaded the bags daily until the moisture evaporated and the roe turned into a kind of cheese. They also preserved salmon roe by curing it in saltwater.

Because species ran at different times (and some might run twice during the year), there were from five to seven major invasions of salmon annually, providing an almost constant supply. To this day, the Indians are closely linked to salmon fishing. In 1974, a federal court decision handed down by Judge George H. Boldt ruled that treaties between Indians and the federal government signed in 1854 had reserved 50 percent of the salmon catch for the tribal signatories. Higher courts have upheld the decision and today salmon fishing in Puget Sound is so strictly regulated that every salmon caught there is labeled Indian or non-Indian.

Salmon is Alaska's most important fish export. The first canneries were opened in 1878, and the fish was long before that a staple food of Alaska's Tinneh Indians. Until recently, most of the roe was exported to Japan, where it is known as *ikura* and is esteemed as a great delicacy. Successful conservation measures in Alaska and British Columbia have increased the harvest in recent years and now Americans are enjoying the processed roe of the Alaskan pink (*Oncorhynchus gorbuschka*) and chum (*O. keta*) salmon. The chum salmon is fished especially for its roe. (*Keta* is Russian for roe, a reminder that the Russians were the first fishermen of the northern Pacific coast.)

To process the roe, the eggs are removed from the sac, separated from the membrane, and pushed through a sieve. They are not graded the way sturgeon are, and the kind of salmon from which the caviar came is never identified. This simplifies the processing procedure, which is reflected in the price of salmon caviar. The roe is agitated in a salt brine for a few minutes, rinsed, and packed in bulk pails for shipment. Salmon caviar is also widely available pasteurized, though as with sturgeon caviar, some textural quality and taste are lost. The color of salmon caviar ranges from golden and reddish amber to reddish orange. The eggs are large (larger than beluga), and the characteristic "pop" as the eggs are rolled between tongue and palate is a surprising and delicious treat. The taste is sharper and more piquant than sturgeon caviar. It is very good spread on toast and in combination with other foods. It has for years been underrated and really deserves the attention of caviar lovers.

Lumpfish and whitefish, cod and carp hold little romance, legend, or mystery. But they do produce a lot of good processed roe. The flesh of the cooked lumpfish has been compared by some to glue pudding and esteemed by others as a feast. The knobby exterior of the fish accounts for its name in English. The chief value of the lumpfish is in the female's roe. The lumpfish is found on both sides of the Atlantic Ocean as well as in the Baltic Sea, most abundantly near Iceland. Most of the roe that finds its way to our markets is caught in Icelandic waters and dyed and pasteurized in Denmark and the United States. Iceland's laws prohibit its export without very heavy salting. For aesthetic reasons, the clear grayish eggs are dyed red, gold, or black, either with vegetable dye or cuttlefish ink, and the roe is usually pasteurized. The dye of this caviar leaking on appetizers has blackened its reputation, and its heavy salting has done nothing to redeem it. Lumpfish benefits greatly by rinsing (see page 34) and, in combination with other foods, can be decorative as well as tasty.

Whitefish from the Great Lakes and Canada is providing an increasingly large share of the processed roe being served in American restaurants and homes. The family Coregonidae is essentially a family of freshwater fish and is known in virtually all northern countries. Fresh golden whitefish caviar is eye-catching: it glistens, shimmers, and glimmers, sometimes appearing iridescent. It is mild though distinctive, crisp, crunchy, and clean tasting. Because of its low oil content and the small size of the individual eggs, this caviar can be frozen successfully. Sturgeon and salmon caviar, on the other hand, will burst and turn to mush when defrosted.

The processed roe of the cod and the carp, though about as different from Caspian sturgeon caviar as mushroom flakes are from truffles, provide some good eating. Cod is probably the world's most important saltwater fish. No other fish can be salted as successfully or keeps longer once it has been so cured. Indeed, it even keeps well without salting, simply dried. In the days before refrigeration, cured cod was in many parts of the world the only fish obtainable at any distance from a coast. The pink roe is a delicacy and is often sold in a pressed and dried form as well as smoked. Flemish fishermen have traditionally taken a large fresh cod's roe and wrapped it in muslin. It is then boiled in salted water, drained, and cooled. The roe is unwrapped, cut into slices, fried, and served on toast. Other fresh roes can also be prepared this way, should you be lucky enough to get some.

The carp, a native of eastern Asia, is perhaps the most important freshwater food fish in the world. Incapable of traversing the barrier of saltwater oceans, the carp was deliberately introduced into other areas where it is found today—Europe, Africa, and North America. It inhabits sluggish waters and prefers areas of tangled vegetation and muddy bottoms. Eastern European housewives sometimes put a live carp in a bathtub filled with fresh water for a few days before cooking it. Alexander Dumas suggested giving the carp a glass of vinegar to drink in order to rid it of its muddy taste. He gave no instructions for persuading the carp to drink the vinegar.

The roes of both the carp and cod are tiny and when salted are often sold in this country as tarama or tarama caviar. In Greece, its home, tarama is made from the roe of the gray mullet, which is its traditional source.

The gray mullet is also the source of another traditional Mediterranean delicacy known as *poutargue* or *boutargue* in France, and *botarga* in Italy. A great and now expensive delicacy, this is the salted, dried, and pressed roe of the gray mullet. (Creating some confusion, *botarga* available in the United States is often the dried, salted roe of tuna. Its preparation and use are the same as for the mullet.) *Poutargue*, or "Provençal caviar" is a specialty of Martigues, near Marseilles. It was known to the people of Crete at the time of Minos and was taken to Provence by Phocaean navigators. Samuel Pepys mentions it in his diary entry for June 6, 1661: "We stayed talking and singing and drinking great draughts of claret, and eating botargo and bread and butter till twelve at night." We can infer that it was a fairly common dish to eat in England. Nowadays, the dish is made almost exclusively in Greece, Turkey, and Italy. In August, when the gray mullet is ready to spawn, she is led into false weirs and speared by fishermen in flat-bottomed boats. The roe is immediately taken from the belly, cleaned, soaked in brine, and dried in the sun. The dried roe can be eaten immediately with bread and oil, although it is usually preserved with a coating of beeswax, which is removed before eating.

The roes of crab, flying fish, cod, and sea urchin are processed and widely used for sushi in Japan. These roes too are becoming available in this country as Japanese cuisine increases in popularity here. The very small, loose salted eggs are often lightly dyed pale orange or yellow to accentuate their color. Crab roe (*masago* in Japanese) has a bittersweet flavor and a crunchy texture, like whitefish roe. Flying fish roe (*tobiko shiozuke*) has a slightly fishy flavor and a very crunchy texture. Cod roe (*ajitsuke tarako*), used widely throughout the world, is almost pastelike and tastes very much like anchovy paste when prepared by the Japanese.

NUTRITIONAL INFORMATION

Caviar isn't just delicious: it is almost good for you. For centuries, caviar was considered an aphrodisiac because of its place in the reproductive process. All fish and their by-products have been linked to the myth of Aphrodite, the goddess of love who was born from the foam of the sea. Supposedly anything that came from the sea would partake of Aphrodite's power. The French prescribe caviar as an antidote to their most common ailment: *crise de foie*. More realistically, perhaps, caviar is considered a remedy for hangovers because it contains acetylcholine, which has been linked to an increased tolerance for alcohol.

Chemical analysis reveals that caviar does contain 47 vitamins and minerals. The caviar proteins, of which there are 122 grams in a pound, include arginine, histidine, isoleucine, lysine, and methionine. The fat in caviar (68 grams per pound) consists of 25 percent cholesterol and 75 percent lecithin. There are 1,188 calories in a pound of caviar; that's only 74 calories per ounce, which is a normal serving. And that is a *real* sixteen-ounce pound, not the fourteen-ounce "pound" in which caviar is retailed and marketed in this country. The discrepancy exists because of the different measuring systems here and in Europe, where the caviar is packed: European tin molds hold 400 grams, which is approximately 14 ounces. The magic of advertising and marketing in this country has translated that into a pound.

Other nutritional information for a pound of caviar includes: 15 grams of carbohydrate; 1,252 milligrams of calcium; 816 milligrams of potassium; and, unfortunately, 9,979 milligrams of sodium. At 623.28 milligrams per one-ounce serving, that is about 100 milligrams more than an ounce of Parmesan cheese and about one-third of the 2,000 milligrams a day recommended by the Senate Select Committee on Nutritional and Human Needs. Sturgeon caviar also provides phosphorus, iron, and traces of vitamins A, C, B2, and B12.

BUYING AND STORING

The ideal fresh sturgeon caviar is plump and moist, with each individual egg shiny, smooth, separate, and softly intact. When you take a spoonful in your mouth and gently press the grains against your palate, they should very briefly resist and then burst to release a vivid flavor—savory, sometimes faintly nutty, with a whiff of the sea but never fishy or salty—surrounded by its own thick natural oils. The caviar should not be swimming in oil or piled high above it. The less salt used in preserving the roe, the truer and better the flavor will be; also the more perishable the caviar. Whether you buy beluga, sevruga, or osetra, caviar labeled "malossol" is preferable. You should buy from a merchant who sells a lot of caviar, has a brisk turnover, and knows how to store it: at between 28 and 32 degrees Fahrenheit, turning the tins continually so the oils are well distributed. A reputable merchant will let you taste what you're buying; just ask. An alternative is to ask for the right to return the caviar if it is unsatisfactory. A retailer should grant it, and the distributor should stand behind the retailer.

The most expensive caviar is not necessarily the best, and even malossol beluga varies in quality from batch to batch. For the "best" the variables had to go in the fish's favor all along the way: the conditions under which the fish grew and spawned, water temperature and salinity, the water's freedom from industrial waste, the age of the fish, and the handling the roe received during all phases of processing, packing, shipping, and storage. There is no "best" sturgeon caviar; what you like best *is* best. Because it is so expensive (and price is partially based on supply and demand), don't fail to ask for a taste before buying. Experience will guide you to making the best choice from the best retailer.

Buy only as much as you plan to eat and make sure it is insulated for the trip home (however short). It should then be stored in your refrigerator, whose normal temperature of around 40 degrees Fahrenheit is a little too warm. The unopened jar or tin can be stored in the refrigerator for four weeks. An opened jar can be stored in the refrigerator, covered, for no longer than two or three days. A noticeable deterioration in quality can be detected as soon as the second day. The caviar is safe to eat though the grains will burst and become watery. Pressed caviar will keep longer. At 40 degrees Fahrenheit it will keep, unopened, for ten days to two weeks. Once opened, you should eat it within five days.

Pasteurized caviar will keep in the refrigerator unopened for several months. White specks of crystallized protein derivatives may begin to appear. Like tartrate crystals in wine, they are harmless, but they do detract from the caviar's visual appeal. Once opened, the pasteurized caviar should be stored like the fresh and consumed within two or three days. There is no mystery to determining if your caviar has gone bad: it will both smell and taste bad.

Fresh salmon caviar, because of its higher salt content, will keep slightly longer than sturgeon caviar. The same cautions apply to it. Buy it and eat it. Over-the-hill salmon caviar will separate, its oil turning to a thin liquid, and it will smell "off." An unfinished container of salmon caviar should be sprinkled with a little tasteless vegetable oil before being covered and stored in the refrigerator.

Whitefish caviar is the only one discussed that can be successfully frozen, though it is most commonly available pasteurized. An opened container will keep refrigerated for about one week or ten days before it turns gritty. As with other roes, it shouldn't be a burden to eat the whole container in one sitting, particularly if you have bought, and invited, carefully.

Lumpfish caviar, which is almost always pasteurized, will keep almost indefinitely in your pantry. Once opened, it will keep for a few weeks, covered, in the refrigerator. Tarama, which can be found in the refrigerated section of the supermarket or specialty store, should be refrigerated at home as well, where it will keep a good long time. An opened jar can be stored for several weeks if it is securely reclosed.

A Note on the Recipes and Cooking with Caviar

The variety of processed fish eggs is vast, the selection and availability are growing, and there is a caviar in every price range. The miracle and the wonder to my mind are not that caviar can be so costly, but that it is commercially available at all, given the hazards of the journey from fish to table.

Don't be timid about making substitutions in the recipes and be adventurous when you are buying caviar. Try all the varieties you can find and ask a fisherman friend or your fishmonger to save roe for you: you can process it yourself (see page 90) or cook it fresh. (Beware, however, of pike roe, which is reputedly toxic.) Shad, haddock, and the coral that is sometimes available with scallops are all delicious. In this book, however, I have limited the recipes to those using processed roes.

One of the keys, indeed perhaps the crucial factor, in preparing tasty food is using the proper amount of salt and pepper. It is always difficult to specify exact quantities, and in this book it is almost impossible because the salt content of the caviar is so wildly variable. I advise you to taste the dish, taste the caviar, and use your best judgment about salt. Be generous with the pepper mill (preground pepper tastes and feels too much like sand to be of any culinary use).

With only a few exceptions, all the recipes in this book call for adding the caviar to a dish at the very last minute, after its cooking is finished. Cooking caviar greatly diminishes its taste and texture, and too much handling makes it mushy. When added at the end, quickly and with a sure hand, it complements the finished dish and adds sparkle and luxury to your table. Its contribution to the finished dish is much greater than the comparatively small quantity usually called for. Caviar has a taste, presence, and texture that make it, in all its varieties, a real treat to eat.

A Word on Quantities: My best judgment, based on experience, on how many people a given quantity of food will feed is stated at the beginning of each recipe. It is impossible to know your guests' appetites and what else will be served with the meal.

HORS D'OEUVRES

The recipes in this chapter are meant to be served predinner, with drinks, or passed at a cocktail party. They have the great advantage of needing only fingers, a napkin, toast, bread, or a crudité; knives, forks, plates, and a steady surface are unnecessary for their comfortable consumption.

illi

"As a young man I had a cozy picture about caviar production. In my mind's eye I saw the broad mouth of a river, which I comfortably called the Malossol; in it a lot of big Russkies, with long beards like in *Boris Godunov*, were singing boat songs and wading and carefully lifting immense sturgeons out of the water while relieving them gently of their eggs with a soft, sluicy swish and then putting them back again, like milked cows let out to pasture. This tableau was in the style and colors of Chagall, and quite pleasant. I ate my caviar in relaxed, uncomplicated gourmand fashion."

LUDWIG BEMELMANS,
Playboy (January 1961)

CAVIAR PUFFS

These are quick to make, delicious to eat, and impressive to serve. The only trick to these puffs is the handling of the pastry bag; but after doing it once or twice, you will master the technique. This recipe can easily be doubled.

MAKES 14–16

½ cup water
4 tablespoons (½ stick)
  butter, cut into small pieces
½ cup unbleached flour

¼ teaspoon salt
2 large eggs
1 egg yolk mixed with
  ½ teaspoon water

Filling

¼ cup heavy cream, whipped
6 tablespoons domestic

sturgeon caviar or golden
  whitefish caviar

1. In a 1-quart saucepan, bring the water and butter to a boil. When the butter is melted, remove the pan from the heat and all at once dump in the flour and the salt. Beat with a large wooden spoon and mix thoroughly. Put the pan back on the heat and beat for 1 or 2 minutes, until the mixture becomes a mass, moves with the spoon, and starts to film the bottom of the saucepan.
2. Remove the pan from the heat for about 5 minutes: the dough should be tepid. Make a well in the center of the dough and break an egg into the well. Beat vigorously until well incorporated. Make another well in the center, and add the second egg. Beat as before for several seconds, making sure you have a smooth dough.
3. Butter a cookie sheet. Preheat the oven to 425 degrees F.
4. Fit the pastry bag with a ½-inch plain tube and fill the bag with the warm *pâte à choux*. Squeeze the dough onto the buttered pastry sheet, making mounds about 1 inch in diameter and ½ inch high. Brush each puff with the egg-water mixture, being careful that

the egg doesn't drip down the sides of the puffs or they may rise unevenly.

5.   Bake in the preheated oven for 20 minutes. The puffs should double in size and be a golden color. Pierce each one with a sharp knife: this will release the steam and prevent the puffs from turning soggy as they cool. Cool the puffs for a few minutes in the turned-off oven with the door ajar, then transfer to a rack until ready to use. The puffs can be frozen at this point. Before serving, put the frozen puffs directly into a 425-degree F. oven for 3 or 4 minutes.

6.   To fill, remove the tops and fill with a spoon. There are several filling possibilities with the ingredients listed above, along with variations below.

Combine the whipped cream with 4 tablespoons of the caviar and spoon ½ tablespoon onto the bottom of each puff. Sprinkle the remaining caviar evenly over the puffs. Cover with the top.

Variations:

8 tablespoons (1 stick) unsalted butter, softened
4–6 tablespoons salmon caviar

1 teaspoon lemon juice
½ teaspoon finely grated lemon zest

1.   Combine all the ingredients in a bowl and fill the bottom halves of the puffs, place the tops on, and refrigerate for 30 minutes before serving.

½ cup sour cream or crème fraîche (see page 31)

3 tablespoons chopped smoked salmon
4 tablespoons salmon caviar

1.   Spread some sour cream or crème fraîche on the bottom of each puff. Top with the chopped smoked salmon and salmon caviar or caviar alone. Cover with the top.

4 ounces (8 tablespoons)	1 hard-boiled egg (see page
cream cheese	39)
1 tablespoon mayonnaise	½ teaspoon commercial white
½ tablespoon sour cream	horseradish, drained
½ tablespoon lemon juice	2 tablespoons salmon caviar

1.   This quantity will fill about 24 puffs. Put everything in a food processor but the caviar. Using the steel blade, make a smooth mixture and transfer to a small bowl. Add the caviar gently and chill for about an hour. With a pastry bag or small spoon, stuff the puffs. Put the tops on and serve.

CRÈME FRAÎCHE

This is so easy to make and so delicious to eat, you should always have some on hand. It can be used wherever sour cream is called for.

| 2 cups heavy cream | 1½ cups sour cream |

1.   Heat the heavy cream in a saucepan until it is lukewarm (85 degrees F.), stirring. It should take about 2 minutes.
2.   Whip the sour cream with a whisk for about 1 minute.
3.   Add the heavy cream to the sour cream and mix well. Cover with a dish towel and leave at room temperature for 12 to 15 hours. You can place the covered bowl in a turned-off gas oven and the process of thickening will be accelerated.
4.   When the mixture is thick, transfer to a screw-top jar and refrigerate. It will keep for 10 days to 2 weeks.

TARAMAKEFTEDES
(Tarama Balls)

These are a delicious and unusual hot hors d'oeuvre. All but the final frying, which takes about 5 minutes, should be done in advance.

MAKES 48

1 pound all-purpose potatoes	½ cup minced parsley
2 tablespoons unsalted butter	2 teaspoons lemon juice
2 tablespoons heavy cream or milk	Freshly ground black pepper
	Flour
1 cup tarama	Vegetable oil, for frying
1 medium onion, coarsely chopped	Parsley sprigs
	Lemon wedges

1. If you happen to have 2 cups of leftover mashed potatoes on hand, use them. Otherwise, scrub the potatoes, quarter them, and put in a medium-size saucepan with cold water to cover. Bring to a boil and cook until the potatoes are soft; time will vary according to the size and type of potatoes used. When the potatoes are done, drain in a colander, peel them, and put back in the saucepan. Over very low heat, add the butter and cream or milk and mash with a wooden spoon or potato masher. Turn off the heat when the butter is melted.

2. Put the potatoes, tarama, and onion into the container of a food processor. Using the steel blade, make a smooth purée. Transfer to a bowl and add the minced parsley, lemon juice, and freshly ground black pepper. Mix well. Refrigerate for at least an hour.

3. Put about ½ cup flour on a large plate and flour your hands. Dip a 1-tablespoon measure into the tarama mixture, filling it only partially, and transfer to the floured palm of one hand. Over the sink, toss the ball from hand to hand, coating it with flour and forming it at the same time. Place the ball on a clean platter and refrigerate when all are made.

4.   Before you are ready to serve, heat ¼ inch vegetable oil in a large, heavy skillet. Fry the balls for about 2 minutes on one side and 1 minute on the other. Don't crowd the pan. Serve immediately with toothpicks on a platter garnished with parsley sprigs and lemon wedges.

NOTE: Leftovers can be frozen and reheated in a 450-degree F. oven for 5 minutes. They are not quite *as* good as freshly made, but certainly good enough to make freezing leftovers more sensible than throwing them out.

NEW POTATOES

Black caviar makes a dramatic color contrast with the potatoes, but then so do golden and red caviars.

SERVES 8–10

1 pound small new potatoes   or domestic sturgeon,
  (about 12)   rinsed and drained black or
½ cup crème fraîche (see   red lumpfish (see page 34),
  page 31) or sour cream   or golden whitefish
4 tablespoons caviar: imported

1.   Scrub the potatoes and put them in a saucepan with cold water to cover. Bring to a boil, lower the heat, and simmer until tender, about 20 minutes.
2.   When the potatoes are cool enough to handle, halve each one. With the small end of a melon-ball scoop, remove the center, leaving at least ¼ inch of potato attached to the skin.
3.   Fill each potato half with a dollop of crème fraîche or sour cream and ¼ to ½ teaspoon of the caviar. Serve warm or at room temperature.

NOTE: You can use the potato centers to thicken a soup or fry them in butter with chopped onion and use to fill an omelette.

LUMPFISH

To remove some of the salt and dye used in processing lumpfish caviar, put a small amount in a small sieve. Lower the sieve into a small bowl of warm water, making sure all the roe is submerged. Leave for two or three minutes; change the water and repeat. Do this three or four times. Finally, drain the lumpfish of all water by letting it rest in the sieve over an empty bowl for five or ten minutes. Gently pat dry with paper towels.

FRIED POTATO SLICES

Quantities are difficult to specify for this hors d'oeuvre because each guest creates his own canapé. Any caviar can be used. You may want to put out an assortment of domestic sturgeon, salmon, golden, and if you can afford it, imported sturgeon caviar, whole or pressed.

SERVES 8–12

7–8 large Idaho potatoes	*Crème fraîche (see page 31)*
Vegetable oil	*or sour cream*
	Caviar

1. Preheat the oven to 375 degrees F.
2. Scrub the potatoes, rub lightly with vegetable oil, and pierce each potato in one or two places with a fork.
3. Bake in the preheated oven for 1 hour.
4. When the potatoes are cool enough to handle, make ¼-inch-thick slices, cutting the potato crosswise. Each slice will be rimmed with skin.

5.   Film a heavy skillet with vegetable oil. Fry the potato slices until golden, turning once. Don't crowd the skillet or the potatoes will steam and not brown properly.

6.   Drain the potato slices on paper towels and arrange on a platter. Serve at room temperature with bowls of crème fraîche and caviar.

POTATO-SKIN SHELLS
FILLED WITH CAVIAR

Caviar's affinity for potatoes goes on and on. For this recipe, use russet potatoes: they are small and have thick skins.

SERVES 8–12

2 pounds small russet potatoes (about 15–20)	*1 cup crème fraîche (see page 31) or sour cream*
Vegetable oil, for frying	*¾ cup golden whitefish caviar*

1.   Preheat the oven to 375 degrees F.

2.   Scrub the potatoes and bake in the preheated oven for 20 to 30 minutes, until tender.

3.   Halve the potatoes lengthwise and scoop out most of the flesh, leaving about ⅛ inch still attached. Save the scooped-out potato for salad or to thicken a soup.

4.   Film a large skillet with vegetable oil and fry the skins, turning them on their sides and over to brown and crisp all over.

5.   Drain on paper towels, hollow side down.

6.   Fill each half with ½ tablespoon of the crème fraîche and 1 teaspoon of the caviar. Serve warm.

CAVIAR CANAPÉS

These canapés look elegant and are delicious. They are a little tricky to make, but don't be discouraged. The result is worth it.

MAKES 36

2 loaves French or Italian
   bread, about 18 inches long
   and 2½ inches in diameter
3–4 tablespoons unsalted
   butter, softened
6 tablespoons minced parsley
2 teaspoons minced onion

6 tablespoons sour cream
3 tablespoons caviar: golden
   whitefish, imported or
   domestic sturgeon, or rinsed
   and drained lumpfish (see
   page 34)

1. Carefully slice the crusts off the breads and make 1-inch-thick slices. With your fingertips, pull out a bit of the center of each piece of bread. Your goal is to make a case for the sour cream and caviar, so make sure some bread remains on the bottom. Butter the rounds on the outside, bottom, and in the hollows. Dip the buttered surfaces, but not the hollow, in minced parsley, using your fingertips, if necessary, to make the parsley adhere.
2. Wrap the minced onion in washed cheesecloth. Pass the package briefly under cold water and squeeze out all the moisture. This technique will diminish the strength of the onion.
3. In a bowl, combine the onion with sour cream. With a small spoon fill the hollows of the bread with the mixture. Top with a dollop of caviar. Refrigerate for a few minutes before serving.

CREAM CHEESE ROLL

8 ounces cream cheese
5 tablespoons chopped chives
4 tablespoons caviar: salmon,
   golden whitefish, or rinsed
   and drained red lumpfish
   (see page 34)

Black bread
Toast points
Trimmed raw vegetables,
   chilled

1. Put the cream cheese on a piece of wax paper about 20 inches long. Cut another piece the same size and place it on top of the cream cheese. With a large rolling pin, roll into a rectangle about ¼ inch thick. Trim the cheese so it is an even rectangle approximately 7 by 11 inches. Chill on the wax paper for about 15 minutes to make it possible to roll the cheese with the filling.

2. Sprinkle the cheese with 4 tablespoons of the chives, leaving a ½-inch border all around. Carefully spread the caviar over the chives.

3. Using a metal spatula and the wax paper as a handle, do a combination roll and fold, starting at the narrow end. Peel off the wax paper as you go along. Make the roll as tight as possible, but not so tight that the caviar oozes out. When the last roll/fold is done, put the cheese, still on its last bit of wax paper, on a counter and invert a serving dish over it. Flip, then peel off the last of the paper. Chill for 30 minutes before serving sprinkled with the remaining chives. Serve with black bread, toast, and/or raw vegetables.

STUFFED CUCUMBER ROLLS

This is a beautiful Japanese-like hors d'oeuvre. Each roll is bordered, top and bottom, with a strip of skin, contrasting dramatically with the pale green of the cucumber flesh.

MAKES 14–16

2 seedless European cucumbers, about 13–14 inches long
4 ounces (8 tablespoons) cream cheese, at room temperature

1 tablespoon minced chives
4 tablespoons golden whitefish caviar or rinsed and drained red lumpfish caviar (see page 34)

1. Slice off the ends of the cucumbers. With a mandoline, swivel-bladed vegetable peeler, or very sharp knife, cut the cucumbers lengthwise into very thin strips, about 11 inches long and 1 to 1½

inches wide. Discard the 2 end slices, which will be green skin only, and the 2 or 3 slices from the central seed core. The yield from each cucumber should be about 7 slices.

2. Mash the cream cheese with the chives.

3. Smear about 1 teaspoon (more on the wider slices) of the cream cheese about ¼ inch from the edge of the cucumber slice. Put a dab of caviar on top of that and roll. The cucumbers should self-seal; if they don't, pierce with a toothpick.

SIMPLE CAVIAR CANAPÉS

There are many simple caviar presentations that will be good to eat, look terrific together on a tray to be served with drinks, and are easily eaten with the fingers. These simple ones can be served with the more elaborate canapés throughout this chapter. Garnish the platter with parsley sprigs, lemon wedges, decoratively cut radishes, carrot curls, or endive leaves.

- Put a teaspoon or so of sturgeon caviar in an empty scrubbed mussel or oyster shell.
- Place a dollop of crème fraîche (see page 31) on an endive leaf and top with caviar.
- Place ½ teaspoon or so of crème fraîche on an ⅛-inch-thick cucumber slice, top with salmon or golden whitefish caviar.
- Cut celery stalks 3 inches long and fill with cream cheese mixed with a little sour cream and minced chives, and top with caviar.
- Put some caviar on hard-boiled egg halves, or with a little sour cream on freshly cooked artichoke bottoms.
- Spread butter on toast points, add a thin layer of smoked cod roe and a dollop of crème fraîche; sprinkle with lemon juice, freshly ground black pepper, and a dill sprig.

HOW TO MAKE GOOD HARD-BOILED EGGS

Properly cooked hard-boiled eggs should be firm but still tender. The dark ring between the yolk and white is harmless but unattractive and can easily be avoided. Place the eggs in a saucepan with cold water to cover. Bring to a boil and cook the eggs at a moderate (not fierce) boil for precisely 12 minutes. Time them from the moment the water comes to the boil. Immediately pour out the boiling water and fill the pan with cold tap water; keep the water running into the pan until it remains cool. Crack the eggs a bit and let stand in the cold water until you are ready to use them.

CAVIAR POUCHES

I first ate these extraordinary caviar-filled crêpes in France, at Le Grand Véfour, Raymond Oliver's splendid restaurant in Paris. He called them *poche à l'aumonière* (beggar's purses). They are superb with imported sturgeon caviar and very good with salmon caviar.

They are the perfect stand-up food because they are picked up with the fingers and consumed in one bite. You may, however, want to serve them as a first course at the table, where food is usually taken more seriously.

MAKES 12

¼ cup milk
4 tablespoons unbleached flour
2 large eggs
Salt
2 tablespoons unsalted butter, melted and cooled

12 long chives or scallion tops
2 tablespoons clarified butter (see page 41)
2 tablespoons crème fraîche (see page 31) or sour cream
4 tablespoons caviar, the best you can afford

1. Combine the milk, flour, eggs, melted butter, and a pinch of salt. Beat with a whisk or wooden spoon to make a smooth batter. Let sit at room temperature for 15 to 30 minutes.

2. Lay the chives in a bowl of hot water for a few seconds, until they are limp. Remove and dry in a single layer on paper towels.

3. In a small seasoned crêpe or omelette pan, no more than 5 or 6 inches in diameter, heat a little of the clarified butter. Dip a standard 2-tablespoon coffee measure into the batter and pour into the heated pan. Immediately rotate the pan, pouring any extra batter back into the bowl. In 10 or 15 seconds, the crêpe will be lightly browned and ready to turn. Use whatever tool you can manipulate easily and quickly to turn the crêpes. I use a chopstick to loosen and remove the crêpe and my fingers to turn it. In another 5 to 10 seconds, the crêpe will be done. Times will vary slightly depending on the heat of the pan. Immediately place the crêpe on a piece of wax paper. Continue making the crêpes, one at a time, adding more butter as necessary. The finished crêpes can be made several hours in advance of serving: stack them between sheets of wax paper and wrap in a plastic bag. Refrigerate.

4. Place ½ teaspoon of the crème fraîche or sour cream in the center of each crêpe and on top of that place 1 teaspoon of the caviar. Gently pleat the crêpe and tie with a chive or scallion top. With clean kitchen shears, cut straight across the top of the pouch, removing any crisp edges and neatening the package; trim the chive. These pouches can be made several hours in advance of serving but must be refrigerated. Bring to room temperature before serving.

5. Just before serving, heat the remaining clarified butter and gently dip the bottom of each pouch in it.

CLARIFIED BUTTER

The milky particles in butter burn first. By clarifying the butter, you remove those particles and can use the butter for frying blinis, omelettes, and other foods that benefit from the taste of butter but need a high temperature to fry properly. When serving melted butter, clarified looks better. Clarifying is a simple procedure and clarified butter will keep, properly stored in a screw-top jar in the refrigerator or freezer, for a long time. Clarify at least a pound at a time, so you always have some on hand.

Slice unsalted butter into 1-inch pieces and put in a saucepan. Melt over low heat and cool for 3 or 4 minutes. Line a sieve with a double layer of cheesecloth that has been washed and squeezed dry. Skim the froth from the butter and pour the remainder through the lined sieve. Leave the milky solids in the bottom of pan (you can enrich a sauce or a soup with this). If some white solids remain, rinse and squeeze the cheesecloth and repeat. Pour into a storage container and refrigerate or freeze until needed. The butter will lose about 25 percent of its volume.

EGGS STUFFED WITH CAVIAR

10 hard-boiled eggs (see page 39)
3½ ounces cream cheese, at room temperature
3 tablespoons sour cream
2 tablespoons minced shallots or scallions
3 tablespoons minced chives

A few drops of Tabasco
Commercial white horse-radish, drained
Dijon mustard
7 ounces rinsed and drained red lumpfish caviar (see page 34)

1.   Halve the eggs lengthwise and force the yolks through a sieve into a bowl. Blend in the softened cream cheese, the sour cream, shallots, chives, and Tabasco. Taste and add a tablespoon or so of drained white horseradish and/or mustard. Gently fold in the caviar.
2.   Using a teaspoon, mound some of the filling in each egg half. Serve at room temperature.

TARAMASALATA

Tarama is salted carp or mullet roe. It is sold in glass jars and is widely available. This salad is quick and easy to make—a matter of five minutes. Serve it as a dip with pita, toast points, celery ribs, cucumber strips, raw thinly sliced turnip, or any other crudité. It is also delicious served on such steamed vegetables as sliced kohlrabi, broccoli, and Brussels sprouts.

4 slices white bread, quartered after crusts removed
½ cup (4 ounces) tarama
3–4 tablespoons fresh lemon juice
½ cup coarsely chopped onion
½–¾ cup olive oil
Chopped parsley
Pitted black olives

1.   Soak the bread in a little water for 2 or 3 minutes. Squeeze out the water and put the bread, tarama, lemon juice, and onion in the container of a blender or food processor. Process or blend for about 1 minute and then, with the motor running, pour in the olive oil in a slow steady stream. The taramasalata should have the consistency of thick mayonnaise. Serve garnished with chopped parsley and olives.

NOTE: The taramasalata will keep, refrigerated, for several days, but should be brought to room temperature before serving.

SOVIET
AND OTHER ROELESS "CAVIARS"

A New York restaurant has on its menu Texas caviar, which is black-eyed peas. Cowboy caviar is a packaged eggplant hors d'oeuvre. There are two kinds of roeless Soviet caviar. One is a synthetic they are allegedly making in the laboratory using proteins, vegetable oil, dyes, and flavorings. This product is, it is rumored, being turned out in factories, like ball bearings.

The other Soviet caviar you can easily make yourself and it's pretty good. For red caviar, put the following ingredients through a meat grinder with large holes so they emerge uniform in size: 1 medium salted herring, cleaned and boned; 2 medium carrots cleaned, with tops removed; 1-inch cube processed cheese; 7 ounces unsalted butter; 1 medium onion; 1 hard-boiled egg (see page 39). Mix and serve garnished with lemon wedges. If you prefer black to red caviar, substitute pitted black olives for the carrots.

VEGETABLE CAVIAR

This recipe and the ones following for mushroom and beet caviars are a tribute to the glory of the word caviar: they contain no fish eggs. They're good, but the only eggs in them are those of a chicken used for garnish.

SERVES 6–10

1 eggplant (about 1 pound)	*Salt*
2–3 green peppers (1 pound, total)	*Freshly ground black pepper*
3 cloves garlic, coarsely chopped	*⅓–½ cup olive oil*
2 tablespoons lemon juice	*2 tablespoons chopped parsley*
1 teaspoon toasted ground cumin seed	*1 hard-boiled egg (see page 39), separated*
Cayenne	*Crudités or toast*
	Niçoise olives

1. Preheat the oven to 400 degrees F.
2. Pierce the eggplant in a couple of places with a fork (to prevent it from exploding in the oven), and place it and the whole peppers in the oven. Roast for 20 minutes, and remove the peppers. Bake the eggplant for an additional 25 to 30 minutes.
3. Remove skin, stem, seeds, and ribs from the peppers. Chop coarsely. Slice the eggplant in half lengthwise and remove the flesh with a spoon. Place the flesh in the container of a blender or food processor. Add the garlic, lemon juice, and green peppers. Process but do not purée; the "caviar" should retain some texture.
4. Add the cumin, a pinch of cayenne, salt, and freshly ground black pepper. With the motor running, slowly pour in the olive oil.
5. Remove to a serving bowl and sprinkle the top with chopped parsley. Force the white and yolk separately through a sieve, forming a decorative pattern around the edge of the bowl. Chill for 2 or 3 hours before serving with crudités or toast, and garnished with olives.

MUSHROOM CAVIAR

The Russians are great mushroom hunters (see *Anna Karenina*), and though they need caviar substitutes less than the rest of the world, they seem to have more recipes for them than anyone else. You won't fool even the caviar innocents, but this dish is very satisfying. Serve with raw vegetables and toast or crackers.

SERVES 4–6

2 tablespoons olive oil
5 tablespoons minced shallots
¾ pound fresh mushrooms,
minced (2½–3 cups)

1 tablespoon minced chives
3 tablespoons sour cream

1. Heat the oil in a sauté pan and add the shallots. Cook slowly for a few minutes to soften, but don't brown the shallots.
2. Add the mushrooms and stir to coat them with the oil and shallots. Cook for 8 to 10 minutes, until the mushrooms are soft. If they give off a lot of liquid, raise the heat for a minute or two and boil off.
3. When the mixture cools a bit, mix in the chives and sour cream.

BEET CAVIAR

This is another Russian creation. Serve it with black bread.

1 tablespoon commercial
white horseradish, drained
One 16-ounce jar beets (9½
ounces beets), drained
½ teaspoon sugar

1 tablespoon white vinegar
2 tablespoons chopped onion
1 tablespoon olive or
vegetable oil

1. Squeeze the liquid out of the horseradish and put it with all the other ingredients into the container of a food processor. Process for a moment or two, but don't purée. In a screw-top jar, this will keep for a week or 10 days in the refrigerator.

CREAM CHEESE AND CAVIAR DIP

This dip is very nice served with trimmed endive leaves, celery, and seeded cucumber strips as well as with crackers or toast points.

4 ounces (8 tablespoons) cream cheese, at room temperature
4 tablespoons crème fraîche (see page 31) or sour cream

2 tablespoons grated onion
Lemon juice
4 tablespoons rinsed and drained red lumpfish caviar (see page 34)

1.   Combine the cream cheese and crème fraîche or sour cream. Mash with a fork until smooth; or use a food processor, running the motor for about 10 seconds.
2.   Add the onion and a few drops of lemon juice. Carefully fold in the caviar and chill.

EGG SALAD WITH CAVIAR

My cousin, Lois Cogen, gave me this recipe. It is simple to prepare and beautiful to look at.

SERVES 6–10

8 hard-boiled eggs (see page 39)
2 tablespoons mayonnaise
1 teaspoon commercial white horseradish, drained
Freshly ground black pepper
½ cup minced red onion

½–⅓ cup sour cream
Minced parsley
7 ounces rinsed and drained red and/or black lumpfish caviar (see page 34)
Toast points
Crudités

1.   Slice the eggs into a bowl and, with a fork, mash with the mayonnaise, horseradish, and some freshly ground black pepper.

2. Put the egg salad in a glass serving bowl, about 5 inches in bottom diameter and 3 inches high. Scatter over the red onion, and with a spatula, smooth on the sour cream.

3. Just before serving, scatter the parsley around the periphery of the bowl and down the center if you are using two colors of caviar. Carefully smooth on the caviar and serve with toast and/or crudités.

SMOKED SALMON CORNETS

2 pounds smoked salmon, thinly sliced and cut into twenty-four 3-inch squares
1 cup heavy cream, whipped
24 endive leaves
12 tablespoons caviar: domestic sturgeon, salmon, or golden whitefish

1. Lay the salmon squares flat on a work surface. Place 1½ to 2 tablespoons whipped cream in the center of each square and roll salmon around it, forming a cone.

2. Place a salmon roll at the wide end of each endive leaf and place ½ tablespoon of the caviar on the tip.

CAVIAR TORTE

SERVES 8 – 10

1 pound (2 cups) cream cheese, at room temperature
4 tablespoons sour cream
3 tablespoons minced parsley
3 tablespoons minced chives
3 tablespoons minced dill
3 tablespoons lemon juice
4 tablespoons chopped
scallions, including some green top
6 tablespoons rinsed and drained red and/or black lumpfish caviar (see page 34)
Minced dill, for garnish
Toast or fresh bread

1. Beat the cream cheese with the sour cream. Add the herbs, lemon juice, and scallions.

2. Line a 2-cup mold, cake pan, or bowl with cheesecloth or wax paper, leaving a large overhang. Add the cream cheese mixture. Cover and refrigerate for 8 to 24 hours.

3. Using the cheesecloth or wax paper as a handle, remove the torte from the mold. Invert on a serving plate and peel off the lining. Mark indentations about ⅛ inch deep and about 1 inch apart along the top. Fill these cavities with caviar, all one color or alternating black and red. Pat the dill around the outside of the torte. Serve with toast or good fresh bread.

STUFFED MUSHROOMS

Draining the yogurt gives it much more body and intensifies the taste. You will be startled by the reduction in volume.

1 cup plain yogurt
12 large mushrooms
2 teaspoons lemon juice
5 tablespoons minced scallions

3 tablespoons rinsed and drained red or black lumpfish caviar (see page 34)
Parsley sprigs

1. Line a fine sieve with washed and squeezed-dry cheesecloth. Add the yogurt and let stand over a bowl for at least an hour. The longer the yogurt stands, the more water will drain out.

2. Remove the mushroom stems and carefully wipe the mushrooms with damp paper towels. Brush them inside and out with the lemon juice.

3. Put the yogurt in a bowl and combine with the minced scallions and the drained caviar. Fill each mushroom with some of the mixture and serve garnished with parsley.

SUSHI

This is very effective when combined with other hors d'oeuvres.

MAKES 16

½ cup rice vinegar
3 teaspoons sugar
4 pieces nori (dried seaweed)
1 cup Japanese rice
One 1-inch-square piece dried
   kelp (kombu)
1 teaspoon sake

Wasabi (Japanese
   horseradish)
3–4 tablespoons caviar
   salmon, rinsed and drained
   red lumpfish caviar (see
   page 34), or crab or flying
   fish roe

1. Combine the rice vinegar and sugar in a small saucepan. Over medium heat, stir until the sugar is dissolved. Cool and refrigerate until you need it: the sushi vinegar will keep for several weeks.
2. Pass the seaweed over a flame to toast lightly; cut in quarters.
3. Put the rice in a colander and run cold tap water over it for a few minutes. The water will drain out as a milky liquid; when the liquid runs clear, set aside to drain for 45 minutes.
4. Put the rice in a saucepan and add 1¼ cups cold water. Add the kelp and bring to a boil. When the water comes to a boil, remove the kelp. Cover the pan and cook at a vigorous boil for 8 or 9 minutes. When all the water is absorbed, pour in the sake, and turn off the heat. Cover the pan with a towel and let stand for 20 minutes.
5. Put the rice in a large mixing bowl and pour in ¼ cup of the sushi vinegar. Mix to combine. At the same time (with the other hand), fan the rice with a piece of cardboard to cool it.
6. Put a piece of the seaweed on a worktable. When the rice is cool to the touch, place about 1 tablespoon in the palm of your hand. Squeeze the rice into an oval and rub a thin layer of wasabi over it. Put the rice oval on the seaweed end nearest you, flush left, leaving a ¼-inch border on the right. Take the bottom edge, and slowly roll closed, using 3 or 4 kernels of rice mashed between your thumb and index finger to seal. Stand the finished roll on a platter, hollow end up. Fill the hollow with ½ to 1 teaspoon of the caviar and serve.

Snail Caviar

A Frenchman, claiming inspiration from a Tibetan lamasery, is farming, harvesting, processing, and selling snails' eggs. Helix Aspera, the small gray (*petit gris*) escargot, is being farmed by an entrepreneur near the Pyrenees in southwest France. Three hundred thousand snails are producing eggs under controlled conditions. Snails are hermaphrodites, so at least there's no need to keep track of the females. Still, they must mate to reproduce. Once a year they mate and twenty days later each partner lays about one hundred eggs, total weight about 3.5 grams (less than ⅛ ounce). The eggs themselves are pinkish gray and about 4 millimeters (1 inch) in diameter, which is larger than beluga. In Paris, where the processed snails' eggs can be bought, they cost more than beluga. The eggs taste like smoky marzipan. The man who is processing them refuses to divulge any of his secrets.

FIRST COURSES

The dishes in this chapter are best served at the table. They need plates, utensils, and a solid surface to be eaten comfortably. Some can easily be served as light entrées.

ıllıı

"There is more simplicity in the man who eats caviar on impulse
than in the man who eats Grape-Nuts on principle."

G. K. CHESTERTON

The Complete
and Classic Caviar Service

*"Fresh caviar, the flavor of which is perfect, does not need any
supplementary condiment."*
—AUGUSTE ESCOFFIER

When you have invested in imported Caspian caviar—malossol
beluga, sevruga, osetra, or pressed—the less you serve with it the less
it is masked and the more you and your guests will enjoy it. The
origin of the ritual of serving caviar with chopped onion, hard-boiled
eggs, capers, sour cream, or whatever else is a mystery. Why diminish
the heady, intense, bewitching experience of eating caviar? What to
eat with caviar is more caviar, toast, blinis, and maybe a touch of
lemon juice, squeezed from a cheesecloth- or linen-wrapped lemon
half, or perhaps a little crème fraîche, the latter particularly with
pressed caviar.

The traditional way to serve fresh caviar is in its tin, with its cover
beside it, in a large shallow bowl of crushed ice. It can also be served
in a *presentoir*, a special caviar server, antique or modern: a glass or
crystal bowl that fits snugly inside a larger silver bowl filled with
shaved ice.

The plates off of which the caviar is to be eaten should be chilled.
There is universal agreement that the caviar should be eaten with a
spoon, so as not to pierce any of the precious eggs which must remain
unbroken until pressed between tongue and palate. What kind of
spoon generates more controversy than the SALT negotiations. One
caviar importer eats his caviar with wooden physicians' tongue de-
pressors; another with the plastic spoons given away in delicatessens
for eating yogurt back at your desk. Silver imparts a metallic taste to
the caviar and the caviar will discolor the silver, as will chicken eggs.
Christian Petrossian, the French caviar importer, has developed a

gold paddle on the end of a soup-spoon-length round handle. Mother-of-pearl, horn, and ivory spoons are other favorites of caviar connoisseurs. No matter what the material, the caviar must be handled gently. Be careful serving it from the tin or glass container to the individual guests.

What to drink with caviar is less controversial than what sort of spoon to eat it with. Iced Russian or Polish vodka or very dry chilled Champagne are the choices. A decorative way to serve the vodka is in a block of ice: put the bottle in an empty half-gallon milk carton. Fill the carton to the neck of the bottle with cold water and store in the freezer. You can, if you like, scatter some flower petals in the water. It will take 12 to 24 hours for the water to freeze into a solid block around the vodka, which itself will not freeze because of its high alcohol content. When you are ready to serve, remove the milk carton by slicing the sides with a knife and peeling the carton away. Be careful serving—the block of ice is slippery.

Toast

The only accompaniments that even caviar snobs allow are blinis (see page 101), crème fraîche with pressed caviar, and toast. To make the toast, buy good-quality packaged white bread. Trim the crusts and slice in half on the diagonal, so triangles are formed. Place the bread in one layer on a baking sheet in a preheated 425-degree F. oven. You can, if you like, brush each slice on both sides with a little melted butter; the buttered slices will cook faster than the unbuttered. Bake the bread for 5 to 8 minutes in the preheated oven, checking to make sure it doesn't become too dark on the botton. Turn and brown on the other side, 2 to 3 minutes. Cool the triangles on a rack and serve with the caviar and unsalted butter.

"The serving of caviar is an elegant ritual at the Pavillon [Henri Soulé's legendary New York restaurant, no longer in business]. All the ingredients are prepared well in advance and brought to the table with split-second timing. The toast arrives warm and the vodka arrives chilled. The unavoidable tray with the collection of nonsense—from harmless shredded whites and yolks of eggs to less harmless chopped onion—is ready. At last the tin is brought in from the pantry where it is kept buried in cracked ice at a temperature of thirty-two degrees. For friends and charter members of the club Soulé often opens a new tin because the eggs might adhere to one another ever so slightly.

"A captain opens the tin, careful not to destroy the beautiful soufflélike structure of the eggs. A waiter stands ready with a plate full of teaspoons.

"Precisely at that moment, the high priest of the caviar cathedral appears behind the altar. He takes half a dozen silver spoons into his left hand, holding them up as a painter holds his brushes. He takes one spoon with his right hand, dips it into the caviar soufflé, and with a fast, resolute, rotating movement of his wrists, somewhat as if he were cutting a Tiffany-made wedding cake, sculptures a large oval form in the shape of a jumbo chicken egg which he carefully places on the plate. He discards the used spoon, takes a new one, repeats the motion, places a second large chicken egg of caviar on the plate. The acolytes, who have been standing motionless, now take over. The captain fills the vodka glass. The high priest still stands there, giving you his benevolent blessing before he fades away. You're alone at last with your magnificent sturgeon's eggs."

JOSEPH WECHSBERG,
Dining at the Pavillon (Little, Brown, 1962)

CAVIAR SOUFFLÉ

All soufflés make a splendid and impressive show. The golden white-fish caviar is small and crunchy and will hold its taste and texture during the cooking. The garnish of crème fraîche and additional caviar is pretty and serves as a sauce.

SERVES 6

5 tablespoons unsalted butter, softened

5 tablespoons unbleached flour

1 cup milk

4 eggs, separated, plus 1 extra white

1 teaspoon grated lemon zest
Salt

8 tablespoons golden white-fish caviar

½ cup crème fraîche (see page 31) or sour cream

1.   Preheat the oven to 450 degrees F.
2.   Use about 1 tablespoon of the butter to lightly grease a 1½- or 2-quart soufflé dish or charlotte mold. Dust the inside of the mold with 1 tablespoon of the flour. Tap out excess and set the mold aside.
3.   In a heavy-bottomed saucepan, heat the milk to about 180 degrees F.; do not boil.
4.   Beat 4 egg yolks until paler in color and thickened.
5.   Sift the remaining 4 tablespoons flour into the yolks and stir until thoroughly combined. Add half the hot milk and the remaining 4 tablespoons softened butter. Stir or beat until smooth.
6.   Scrape the mixture through a sieve into a saucepan. Add the remaining milk and the lemon zest. Beat constantly over low heat until the soufflé base is thick. Remove from the heat.
7.   Beat the 5 egg whites with a pinch of salt until soft peaks form. Stir about ⅓ of the whites into the soufflé base. Quickly but lightly fold in the rest of the egg whites and 4 tablespoons of the caviar. Pour the mixture into the prepared soufflé dish or mold.
8.   Place in the preheated oven. After 10 minutes, reduce the heat to 400 degrees F. Run a knife around the edge of the soufflé dish,

quickly cutting down and entirely around. This will allow the soufflé to rise more without spilling over the sides.

9. Bake another 5 to 10 minutes and serve immediately, garnishing each serving with crème fraîche and the remaining caviar.

ANCHOVY SOUFFLÉ WITH COD ROE SAUCE

SERVES 6–8

4 cups milk
5 tablespoons butter
2 tablespoons minced onion
5 tablespoons flour
Salt

Freshly ground black pepper
6 ounces anchovy fillets
4 eggs, separated, plus one
   extra white

Cod Roe Sauce

½ cup heavy cream
2 tablespoons minced chives

2 tablespoons smoked cod roe
   paste

1. You will need cooled béchamel sauce for both the soufflé and the sauce, so start with that. Scald the milk and let it cool. Melt the butter in a heavy saucepan over low heat. Add the onions, and cook for 4 or 5 minutes, until the onion is soft but not brown. Stir in the flour and cook, stirring constantly, for 5 minutes. Remove the pan from the heat and pour in the cooled scalded milk, whisking until the mixture is thick and smooth. Add salt cautiously and freshly ground black pepper. Simmer the sauce for 15 minutes. Strain through a fine sieve into a bowl. Cover with a buttered round of wax paper.

2. Preheat the oven to 375 degrees F.

3. Force the anchovies along with 2 teaspoons of oil from the tin through a sieve; or process for a moment in a food processor.

4. Beat the egg yolks until they are paler and thicker. Stir in the anchovies and combine with 2 cups of the cooled béchamel.

5. Beat the egg whites with a pinch of salt until stiff peaks form. Stir about ⅓ of the whites into the anchovy mixture and gently fold in the rest.

6. Transfer the soufflé mixture to a buttered 1½-quart soufflé dish or charlotte mold. Put the mold in a larger pan and add enough hot water to reach 2 inches up the sides of the soufflé dish. Bake in the preheated oven for 25 minutes. The soufflé should be puffed and golden on top and just done inside.

7. While the soufflé is cooking, make the Cod Roe Sauce. Add the heavy cream to the remaining cup of béchamel and heat gently, stirring. Off the heat, stir in the chives and smoked cod roe paste. Pass the sauce with the soufflé.

STEAK TARTARE

This is a quite luxurious version of a classic dish. If you are feeling generous and are willing to share, this quantity will feed two or three people as an appetizer, and one as an indulgent entrée.

1 egg yolk
Salt
Freshly ground black pepper
Paprika
½ teaspoon Dijon mustard
1 teaspoon Worcestershire sauce
1 tablespoon olive oil
2 tablespoons minced onion
1 tablespoon chopped capers

1 tablespoon lemon juice
1 tablespoon Cognac
1 tablespoon minced parsley
7–8 ounces finely minced or coarsely ground filet mignon
2 tablespoons caviar: beluga, sevruga, or osetra
Toast

1. In a small bowl, mix the egg yolk, a pinch of salt, some freshly ground black pepper, a pinch of paprika, mustard, and Worcestershire sauce. Slowly whisk in the oil. Add the onion, capers, lemon juice, Cognac, and parsley. Combine with the meat and top with the caviar. Serve with buttered toast.

CAVIAR MOUSSE

SERVES 6

1 tablespoon vegetable oil
1 envelope powdered gelatin
½ cup milk
1 cup heavy cream, whipped
⅔ cup mayonnaise

1 tablespoon lemon juice
6–8 tablespoons rinsed and
*   drained red lumpfish caviar*
*   (see page 34)*
Lettuce

1. Lightly oil a 1-quart plain or decorative mold with vegetable oil.
2. In a saucepan, sprinkle the gelatin over the cold milk and heat gently, stirring until the gelatin dissolves, about 2 or 3 minutes. Cool to room temperature.
3. To the cooled milk, add the whipped cream, mayonnaise, and lemon juice. Beat for a moment. Fold in the caviar and pour into the mold. Tap gently on the counter to distribute the mixture evenly.
4. Cover the mold with plastic wrap and refrigerate for 4 hours. To unmold, dip the outside into hot water and turn out onto a platter lined with lettuce leaves.

SALMON-AND-CAVIAR-STUFFED AVOCADO

SERVES 6

1 pound fresh salmon fillet
*   or smoked salmon*
2 tablespoons lemon juice
2 tablespoons mayonnaise
2 tablespoons sour cream

1 tablespoon grated onion
½ tablespoon commercial
*   white horseradish, drained*
3 ripe, unblemished avocados
4 tablespoons salmon caviar

1. Dice the salmon, removing any skin and bones. You will have about 1½ cups. Place in a bowl and add 1 tablespoon of the lemon juice. Let sit for 5 to 10 minutes.
2. Add the mayonnaise, sour cream, grated onion, and horseradish to the salmon. Mix well. Refrigerate until ready to serve, up to 3 hours.

3.   Just before serving, halve the avocados and brush the exposed flesh with the remaining lemon juice. Gently stir 3 tablespoons of the caviar into the salmon. Fill each half with 1½ to 2 tablespoons of the salmon-caviar mixture and garnish each half with ½ teaspoon caviar.

AVOCADO MOUSSE

The colors of this mousse are serene and comforting, as is the taste.

SERVES 6−8

2 large avocados
2−3 tablespoons lemon juice
1 teaspoon salt
1 teaspoon ground coriander
3 tablespoons grated onion
1 envelope powdered gelatin

2 tablespoons mayonnaise
⅔ cup heavy cream
Lime slices
4 tablespoons golden white-
* fish caviar*

1.   Peel the avocados and discard any blemished spots. Place in a blender or food processor container with the lemon juice, salt, coriander, and onion. Make an absolutely smooth purée. You should have about 2 cups.
2.   Soften the gelatin in ¼ cup cold water. Heat, but don't boil, to dissolve. Cool to room temperature.
3.   Combine the avocado purée with the gelatin and the mayonnaise. Refrigerate for 15 minutes.
4.   Beat the cream until stiff, and fold into the avocado. Place in a 1-quart plain or decorative mold. Refrigerate for at least 8 hours.
5.   To serve, run a sharp knife around the edge of the mold. Place a small platter over the mold and invert. Place a dish towel, soaked in hot water and squeezed so it isn't dripping wet, over the bottom of the mold. Shake a couple of times, tap once or twice with a wooden spoon, and lift off the mold. Decorate the sides of the mousse with lime slices and cover the top with caviar. Serve in wedges or slices.

MOUSSELINE OF SMOKED SALMON AND CAVIAR

This mousse is a gorgeous pink color which contrasts most pleasingly with the smoked salmon and parsley. While the recipe calls for smoked salmon, it can be made with inexpensive smoked salmon ends and trimmings.

SERVES 6–8

1½ pounds smoked salmon (1 pound of ends; ½ pound should be sliced very thin)

¼ cup sour cream

8 tablespoons (1 stick) unsalted butter

4–6 tablespoons salmon caviar

4 tablespoons minced parsley

1. Dice 1 pound of the salmon, discarding any skin, bones, and cartilage.

2. Put the salmon in a food processor fitted with the steel blade and add the sour cream and butter. Purée until absolutely smooth.

3. Butter a 1-quart loaf pan and line the pan with wax paper. Trim the wax paper so it fits smoothly; any folds or creases will mar the appearance of the finished mousse.

4. Use half the sliced smoked salmon to line the bottom of the loaf pan. Slightly overlap the slices and run them up the short sides if they are long enough. Fill the pan with half the purée. Gently smooth the caviar over the purée and cover with the remaining smoked salmon purée. Finally, lay the remaining slices of smoked salmon over the top, overlapping again. Cover and refrigerate overnight.

5. To serve, run a flat metal spatula between the wax paper and the edge of the pan, on all four sides. Invert the pan over a small platter, tap a few times with a wooden spoon, and lift off the loaf pan. Remove the wax paper. Decorate the edges of the mousse with the minced parsley, letting some fall to the plate to surround the mousseline. Serve with toast or good French bread.

MARINATED RAW FISH WITH BOTARGA

The salty and pungent taste of *botarga* (dried tuna roe) is wonderful with the raw fish. This dish can be served as a first course or as a luncheon entrée.

SERVES 4–6

½ pound salmon fillet
½ pound flounder, sole, or
   striped bass fillets
3 tablespoons botarga
5 tablespoons lemon juice
12 black peppercorns

Fresh tarragon or parsley
4 tablespoons olive oil
Cucumber slices
4 tablespoons golden whitefish caviar or salmon caviar
Lemon wedges

1. Chill a platter.
2. Slice the fillets as thin as possible, on a diagonal. Discard any skin and bones.
3. Lay the fish slices on the chilled platter, alternating the colors. Sprinkle the *botarga* evenly over the fish.
4. Pour the lemon juice over the fish, completely covering the slices. Scatter the peppercorns over and sprinkle with tarragon or parsley. Cover and refrigerate for at least 30 minutes or up to 2 hours.
5. Just before serving, dribble the olive oil over the fish. Place the cucumber slices in the center of the platter and top them with the caviar. Surround the dish with lemon wedges.

SMOKED SALMON BISCUITS WITH CAVIAR

These can be passed with drinks or served, three or four halves to a plate, as a first course.

MAKES 12–14

1 cup unbleached flour
1 teaspoon double-acting baking powder
Salt
2 tablespoons unsalted butter, chilled
½ cup heavy cream
3 ounces smoked salmon, diced

2 tablespoons chopped dill
1 tablespoon milk
½ cup crème fraîche (see page 31) or sour cream
6–8 tablespoons salmon caviar
Dill sprigs

1. Preheat the oven to 400 degrees F.
2. In the bowl of a standing mixer, combine the flour, baking powder, a pinch of salt, and butter. Mix at medium speed until the mixture resembles coarse meal. Slowly add the heavy cream. The dough should be soft and maleable. Add 1 or 2 tablespoons more cream, if necessary. Stir in the smoked salmon and the dill, reserving some dill for garnish.
3. Put the dough on a floured surface and, with heel of your hand, pat it out into a circle, roughly 9 inches in diameter and ½ inch thick.
4. Use a 2- to 3-inch decorative cookie cutter to make the biscuits. Transfer each to a lightly buttered cookie sheet. Combine and reroll the scraps until all the dough is used.
5. Brush the top of each biscuit with milk and bake in the preheated oven for 15 to 20 minutes. They should be golden brown and puffed.
6. Halve the biscuits horizontally and put a teaspoon of the crème fraîche on each half; top with a teaspoon of the caviar and a dill sprig.

SALMON MOUSSE WITH
CAVIAR MOUSSELINE SAUCE

SERVES 6–8

*1 pound salmon, poached or
   canned*
5 tablespoons white wine
*4 tablespoons chopped
   scallions or shallots*
½ cup heavy cream
¼ teaspoon salt

*¼ teaspoon freshly ground
   white pepper*
⅛–¼ teaspoon cayenne
3 eggs
*½ cup chopped fresh sorrel
   or spinach*

Caviar Mousseline Sauce

2 egg yolks
4 teaspoons lemon juice
6 tablespoons unsalted butter

½ cup heavy cream, whipped
4 tablespoons salmon caviar

1.   Preheat the oven to 400 degrees F.
2.   If using leftover or freshly poached salmon, pick over and discard the bones, skin, and fat. If using canned salmon, drain, reserving the liquid, and discard the skin and bones.
3.   Put the salmon and either wine or liquid from the can into the container of a food processor fitted with the steel blade. Add the remaining ingredients, except the sorrel or spinach. Process until perfectly smooth.
4.   Pour half the mixture into a lightly oiled 1-quart mold or loaf pan. Gently lay the sorrel or spinach on top. Cover with the remaining mousse. Place the pan in a larger pan filled with boiling water to reach ¾ the way up the sides of the mold. Place in the preheated oven and bake for 30 minutes, or until the mousse is firm to the touch. Remove from the water and cool. Unmold and chill for several hours before serving, sliced, with the Caviar Mousseline Sauce.

5.   To make the sauce, using the proportions given above, follow the technique for Hollandaise Sauce on page 125. Just before you are ready to serve, fold the whipped cream and caviar into the sauce. The sauce can be made in advance and kept warm as instructed, but it will liquify if you fold the whipped cream in too soon.

SMOKED SALMON ROLLS
FILLED WITH CAVIAR WHIPPED CREAM

This is a very elegant and very delicious first course. Serve two or three to a plate.

SERVES 4 – 6

½ pound smoked salmon,   *½ cup heavy cream, whipped*
*   sliced not quite paper thin*   *2 teaspoons commercial white*
*   into 12 slices roughly*   *   horseradish, drained*
*   4 inches by 2 inches*   *4 tablespoons salmon caviar*

1.   If your salmon slices are longer and thinner than those specified above, fold them in half lengthwise in an overlapping V.
2.   Whip the cream until stiff. Add the horseradish, drained and squeezed dry of its vinegar brine.
3.   Finally, gently combine the caviar with the whipped cream.
4.   Place about ½ tablespoon of the cream mixture on each slice of smoked salmon: if the piece will hold more, use more. Fold rather than roll the slices around the cream. The salmon should completely enclose the cream. You can serve immediately or refrigerate for several hours.

CAVIAR-STUFFED BAKED POTATO

Diamond Jim Brady is said to have mashed a pound of Hudson River sturgeon caviar into each baked potato he ate, and he ate several a week.

SERVES 6

6 large Idaho potatoes
6 tablespoons unsalted butter
½ cup crème fraîche (see page 31) or sour cream
1 teaspoon finely grated lemon zest
Salt
Freshly ground black pepper

4 tablespoons chopped chives
6 tablespoons caviar: fresh or pasteurized sturgeon caviar, domestic or imported would be exquisite as would pressed caviar; but salmon or golden whitefish would also be very good

1. Preheat the oven to 400 degrees F.
2. Scrub the potatoes, pierce each one with a fork, and bake for 1 to 1¼ hours.
3. When done, hold the hot potato with a potholder and cut a horizontal slice, about ½ inch thick from the top. You can leave the slice attached or remove it. Without piercing the skin, scoop out the potato pulp—a serrated curved grapefruit knife, along with a teaspoon, is useful for this operation. Put the potato pulp in a saucepan and the skins back in the turned-off oven.
4. To the potato pulp, add the butter, crème fraîche, lemon zest, salt, and freshly ground black pepper. Stir over low heat to combine and break up lumps. A large wooden spoon or an old-fashioned potato masher are both useful. Add more butter and/or sour cream if you prefer a creamier texture. Off the heat, add the chives.
5. Stuff the potato skins with the mixture. Top each with 1 tablespoon of the caviar, put on the top, and serve.

Variation: Mash the baked potato and combine with ⅓ cup finely chopped onion, ½ cup (or enough to bind the potatoes) sour cream, 6 tablespoons tarama, and freshly ground black pepper. Fill the potato shells with the mixture.

CAVIAR ROULADE

This elegant presentation can be assembled and refrigerated for an hour or so before serving, at room temperature.

SERVES 8

4 tablespoons (½ stick) unsalted butter
½ cup unbleached flour
2 cups hot milk
4 eggs, separated
Salt

3 ounces cream cheese at room temperature
1 cup crème fraîche (see page 31) or sour cream
2 tablespoons chopped chives
6–8 tablespoons salmon caviar

1. Preheat the oven to 325 degrees F.
2. Melt the butter in a medium-size, heavy-bottomed saucepan over gentle heat.
3. With some of the melted butter, grease an 11-by-16-inch jellyroll pan. (You can also use a 10-by-15-inch jellyroll pan. Do not use anything larger than the 11-by-16-inch pan or the roll will be too thin and too brittle to roll properly.) Line the pan with wax paper, going up the sides, Brush with additional melted butter, and sprinkle lightly and evenly with flour, tapping out excess.
4. Add the ½ cup flour to the warm butter, stirring with a whisk. Over low heat, continuing to stir, slowly add the milk. Cook until thickened and smooth. Simmer, still stirring, for 2 minutes.
5. Beat the egg yolks for a minute or two and, still beating, slowly add the hot sauce to them. Continue beating until all lumps are dissolved.
6. Beat the egg whites with a little salt until stiff peaks form. Stir about ⅓ of the whites into the base. Gently fold in the remaining whites.
7. Spread the batter in the prepared pan, gently smoothing the top with a spatula.
8. Bake in the preheated oven for 30 to 40 minutes. The roll should be golden on top and spring back to the touch.

9.   Remove from the oven and turn out onto a dish towel. After 5 minutes, peel off the wax paper. Cover with another dish towel, this one damp, to keep the roll pliable.

10.   Make the filling by beating together with a hand mixer or in a standing electric mixer, the cream cheese with 4 tablespoons of the crème fraîche or sour cream. Gently add half the caviar.

11.   Remove the top dish towel and spread the cheese-caviar over the roll, leaving a 1-inch border all around. Roll from the narrow end, just like a jellyroll.

12.   Trim the edges. Smear the remaining crème fraîche–cream cheese mixture over the roll, hiding any cracks. Scatter the chives all over the top of the roll. Spread with the remaining caviar.

GINGER-CAVIAR MOUSSE

SERVES 6

1 envelope powdered gelatin	*Salt*
3 hard-boiled eggs (see page 39)	*2 tablespoons lemon juice*
1 tablespoon chopped onion	*¼ cup mayonnaise*
1 tablespoon coarsely chopped ginger	*4 tablespoons rinsed and drained red lumpfish caviar (see page 34)*

1.   Soften the gelatin in 4 tablespoons cold water. Heat to dissolve, but don't boil. Cool to room temperature.

2.   Place eggs, onion, ginger, a pinch of salt, and lemon juice in the container of a processor or a blender. Purée. Combine with cooled gelatin and mayonnaise. Gently stir in the caviar.

3. Turn into a 2-cup mold or individual small molds. Refrigerate for several hours before serving. To unmold, run a sharp knife around the edge of the mold. Place a small platter or individual serving plate over the mold and invert. Place a dish towel, soaked in hot water and squeezed so it isn't dripping wet, over the bottom of the mold. Shake a couple of times and lift off the mold.

SEVICHE WITH AVOCADO AND SALMON CAVIAR

This is not the classic, highly spiced seviche, but a mild dressing to "cook" the fish and not distract from the intensity of the caviar.

SERVES 6

3 tablespoons fresh lime juice	a firm white fish such as
Freshly ground white pepper	flounder, or bay scallops
Salt	2 ripe avocados
2 tablespoons minced shallots	4 tablespoons salmon caviar
7 tablespoons olive oil	Parsley sprigs
1 pound sea scallops, fillet of	Lime wedges

1. In a small bowl combine the lime juice with a few grindings of white pepper, a little salt, and the shallots. Slowly whisk in the olive oil.
2. Chop the sea scallops or the flounder; bay scallops should be left whole. Dry the fish between several layers of paper towels. Combine with half the dressing and let sit for about 30 minutes at room temperature, longer in the refrigerator.
3. Peel and halve the avocados and slice ¼ inch thick.
4. Put the scallops in the center of a platter and arrange the avocado slices decoratively around them. Brush the avocado with the remaining dressing. Scatter the caviar over the scallops. Arrange the parsley and lime wedges around the platter and serve.

CAVIAR PIE

SERVES 6

6 hard-boiled eggs (see page 39)
2 tablespoons mayonnaise
3–4 tablespoons minced scallions, including 2 inches of green top
3½ ounces rinsed and drained red or black lumpfish caviar (see page 34)

1 teaspoon grated lemon peel
1 cup sour cream
4 tablespoons chopped chives
6 paper-thin lemon slices, halved, to yield 12 half-moons
Black olives

1.   Crack and peel the hard-boiled eggs.

2.   Chop the eggs coarsely and mash them through a sieve into a bowl. Add the mayonnaise and minced scallions, combining well.

3.   Press this "crust" into an 8-inch cake or pie tin. Use your fingers to spread the eggs up the side and evenly across the bottom. Refrigerate for 8 hours.

4.   Spread the rinsed and drained lumpfish over the eggs. Sprinkle with lemon peel. Carefully spread the sour cream over the lumpfish. You will inevitably stir some of the lumpfish into the sour cream.

5.   Cover the top of the pie with the chopped chives or scallion tops. Place the lemon slices around the edges, punctuated with black-olive halves.

"There are many pleasant things to be done with caviar, by people who respect the intrinsic fact that it must and can stand alone, unaided and unstretched by such deceivers as minced onion, chopped hard eggs, strips of anchovy. Perhaps the most impressive such thing I have eaten is a caviar pie made by an amateur chef. . . . The pie is a gem of simplicity: a baked pastry shell, filled with about a quart of commercial sour cream stiffened with one tablespoon of dissolved gelatin and delicately seasoned with minced chives, and then a half pound, or more of good fresh caviar spread evenly over. Come the Revolution . . ."

M. F. K. FISHER,
With Bold Knife and Fork (Putnam's, 1968)

SOUPS

The caviar adds taste, beauty, and textural interest to these soups as well as elegance to the presentation. Even the lowly (and delicious) lentil soup becomes festive with the addition of caviar. The caviar will sink in the soup if a "raft" isn't provided. In most of these recipes I recommend a lemon slice or a dollop of sour cream or an egg-white island be floated on top of the soup to prevent the caviar from disappearing to the bottom.

॥||

" 'I've never understood such reverence for fish eggs,' the wife
of the Canadian ambassador said, shaking her head and
laughing.
"James looked at her over half-glasses. 'Fish eggs? Rather
God's gift to the educated palate.' "

MARGARET TRUMAN,
Murder on Embassy Row (Arbor House, 1984)

CREAM OF SCALLOP SOUP

This soup is wonderful, hot or cold.

SERVES 5 – 6

1 ½ cups dry white wine or
    dry white vermouth
2 ½ cups water
¾ pound potatoes, peeled
    and coarsely chopped
    (1 ½–2 cups)
1 cup chopped onion
½ cup sliced carrots
¼ teaspoon dried thyme
¼ teaspoon fennel seed
1 clove garlic, mashed with
    the handle of a knife

6 parsley sprigs tied together
    in washed cheesecloth with
    half a bay leaf
1 pound (2 cups) sea scallops,
    quartered
2 egg yolks
½ cup heavy cream
½ cup milk
4 tablespoons golden white-
    fish caviar

1. In a partially covered saucepan, simmer together for 30 to 40 minutes, or until the potatoes are soft, all the ingredients up to the scallops. Add the scallops and cook for 2 to 3 minutes.

2. Discard the parsley and bay leaf, and pass the soup through a food mill or purée in a blender or food processor.

3. In a small bowl, combine the yolks with the cream.

4. Return the soup to the heat and bring just to the simmer. Slowly beat about 2 cups hot soup into the yolk-cream mixture. Then slowly pour back into the soup pan, whisking as you do. If the soup is too thick, add the milk. Don't boil, just heat the soup. Serve immediately, garnished with the caviar. To serve the soup chilled, cool after the egg yolks and cream have been combined with the soup. Chill for several hours, adding milk just before serving if the soup seems too thick.

COLD MUSHROOM SOUP
WITH FLOATING ISLANDS
À LA JACQUES MAXIMIN

This spectacular cold soup is an adaptation of a quite elaborate and impressive soup served by Maximin at the Chanticleer, his restaurant in the Negresco Hotel in Nice.

SERVES 6

9 ounces mushrooms
4 tablespoons (½ stick)
  unsalted butter
½ tablespoon lemon juice
Cayenne
Salt
Freshly ground black pepper
3 egg whites

1 cup heavy cream
2 tablespoons chopped chives
6 tablespoons the best black
  caviar you can afford:
  imported or domestic sturgeon, or rinsed and drained
  lumpfish (see page 34)

1.   Trim the mushrooms and wipe them clean with damp paper towels. Quarter them and place in a medium-size, heavy-bottomed saucepan with 1 quart water, the butter, lemon juice, a pinch of cayenne, and a little salt and freshly ground black pepper. Bring to the boil and cook briskly for 5 minutes. Put the slightly cooled solid contents of the pan into the container of a blender or food processor. Purée and then pass through a fine sieve. Recombine with the liquid and chill.

2.   About an hour before you plan to serve, heat to about 170 degrees F. 4 quarts of lightly salted water in a large, shallow skillet with a wide diameter. Don't boil the water.

3.   Beat the egg whites with a pinch of salt until they form stiff peaks. Dip 2 tablespoons in cold water (and redip in cold water after each "island" is made) and make 12 floating islands in the shape of small sausages. Poach them in the hot water for 6 or 7 minutes. Cook the islands in batches if your skillet won't accommodate

them all at once, but do not crowd the pan. Remove carefully with a slotted spoon and drain on paper towels.

The first islands might look messy. As you make them, you will go faster and make neater ones. In any case, even the least appealing in the poaching water will look spectacular in the soup.

4.   Beat the cream until stiff. Fold it quickly into the chilled soup and season with salt, pepper, and additional cayenne if the soup needs it. Divide the soup among 6 chilled soup bowls and sprinkle with chopped chives. Float 2 egg-white islands into each bowl and carefully place ½ tablespoon of the caviar on top of each.

VICHYSSOISE

This soup is very easy to prepare. It will keep refrigerated for about five days and is very nice to have on hand, particularly in summer. It can be frozen after step 3.

SERVES 12

1½ pounds potatoes, peeled and diced (about 3–4 cups)
4 cups sliced leeks, including 1–2 inches of green top
9 cups water
1 tablespoon salt
1 cup heavy cream

6 tablespoons minced chives or parsley
6 tablespoons crème fraîche (see page 31) or sour cream
6 tablespoons salmon caviar or golden whitefish caviar

1.   Put the potatoes, leeks, water, and salt in a large saucepan. Bring to a simmer and cook, partially covered, for 45 minutes.
2.   Purée through a food mill or in a blender or food processor.
3.   Beat in the heavy cream and chill.
4.   Ladle the soup into chilled bowls. Sprinkle the surface of each bowl with minced chives or parsley. Float a dollop of crème fraîche or sour cream in the center of each bowl, and place ½ tablespoon of the caviar on top of that.

COLD AVOCADO SOUP

SERVES 6

3 large avocados, about ¾
    pound each
2 teaspoons lemon juice
1 tablespoon grated onion
1 cup chicken stock
1 cup water
½ cup sour cream

½ cup heavy cream
Freshly ground white pepper
1 teaspoon salt
6 tablespoons golden white-
    fish caviar
Lime slices

1. Peel 2 of the avocados, chop coarsely, and place in the container of a food processor with the lemon juice and grated onion. Make a smooth purée. You will have about 1½ cups.

2. Put the purée in a bowl, and with a whisk, beat in the chicken stock, water, sour cream, heavy cream, a few grindings of white pepper, and the salt.

3. Chill the soup and 6 soup bowls.

4. To serve, peel the third avocado. Make the slices the full length of the bulb end. Chop any avocado flesh that remains on the pit. Sprinkle the chopped avocado over the soup and float the slices over that. Place 1 tablespoon of the golden caviar on each avocado slice, garnish the bowls with lime slices, and serve.

OYSTER VELOUTÉ WITH BLACK CAVIAR

Paula Wolfert developed this recipe—basing it on the traditional cooking of southwest France—and published it in *The Cooking of South-West France* (Dial, 1983).

In that part of France, the Gironde River provides the caviar and the Bay of Arcachon the oysters. This is a wonderful, smooth soup, elegant and delicious.

SERVES 6–8

2 shallots, peeled and finely chopped

3 tablespoons unsalted butter

3 tablespoons all-purpose flour

3 cups unsalted fish stock

3 cups unsalted chicken stock, degreased

¾ teaspoon sea salt

12–15 oysters, shucked, plus their clear liquor

Cayenne

3 large egg yolks

¾–1 cup heavy cream

2–3 tablespoons imported or domestic sturgeon caviar, or rinsed and drained black lumpfish caviar (see page 34)

Lemon juice

1. In a 4-quart heavy-bottomed saucepan, soften the shallots in the butter without browning. Blend in the flour and cook over low heat, stirring often, for 10 minutes. This roux must be very smooth and not darken beyond the color of yellow straw; it must cook slowly so the flour proteins will absorb the liquid.
2. In a second saucepan, combine the stocks and heat to lukewarm. Gradually add to the roux, stirring constantly, and bring to a boil over medium heat. Reduce heat and simmer for 20 minutes, skimming the surface. Add half the sea salt.
3. Strain the oyster liquor to remove any traces of shell and sand. Purée the oysters in a food processor or blender. Add puréed oysters and strained liquor to soup. Simmer, partially covered, for 5 minutes. Add a pinch of cayenne. Rub the soup through a fine sieve set over

a large mixing bowl, pressing down hard with the back of a spoon to extract as much oyster pulp as possible.

4.   Just before serving, reheat the soup. Combine the egg yolks and ¾ cup of the heavy cream in a small mixing bowl; whisk them together. Gradually beat in 1 cup of the hot soup. Stir the egg-yolk mixture back into the hot soup and continue stirring constantly over low heat, until the soup has thickened slightly. Bring the soup to just below the boil. Remove from the heat and taste for seasoning, adding more cream and the remaining salt if necessary. Ladle the soup into warmed soup bowls and top each with a teaspoon of the black caviar. Sprinkle with a few drops of lemon juice and serve immediately.

NOTE: To serve the soup cold, chill quickly over ice water, then refrigerate. Thin with heavy cream and milk before serving with caviar and lemon juice.

LENTIL SOUP

This is a hearty, filling soup. Along with a salad and bread and butter, it makes a splendid lunch.

SERVES 8–10

½ pound salt pork or bacon, chopped
1 tablespoon unsalted butter
2 cups chopped leeks, including a few inches of green top
1 cup chopped carrots
1 cup chopped celery, plus 2 tablespoons coarsely chopped celery leaves
1 pound (2 cups) lentils

2 bay leaves, 5 black peppercorns, ½ teaspoon dried thyme, tied together in cheesecloth
3 tablespoons lemon juice
Grated zest of 1 lemon
1 cup minced scallions
20 thin lime slices
1 cup sour cream
10 tablespoons salmon caviar

1. In a large, heavy saucepan, sauté the salt pork or bacon in the butter for 5 minutes. Add the chopped leeks, carrots, celery, and celery leaves. Sauté gently, until the vegetables soften, about 10 minutes.

2. Wash the lentils in a sieve under cold tap water. Add to the vegetables along with 10 cups water and the herbs in the cheesecloth bag. Bring to a boil; then partially cover, lower the heat, and simmer for 30 minutes.

3. Discard the cheesecloth and purée the soup in a food mill or processor. Return to the saucepan and add the lemon juice and zest. Reheat and serve in individual bowls, sprinkled with minced scallions. Place 2 lime slices in each bowl. Put a dollop of sour cream in the center of each bowl, between the lime slices, and a tablespoon of the caviar on top of that.

CHLODNIK

This iced Russian soup combines an assortment of ingredients that together approximate *kvas*, a fermented barley liquor that is the key ingredient in the Russian version. The soup should be served as cold as possible, in chilled bowls.

SERVES 8–10

4 cucumbers
Coarse salt
1 pound bulk or packaged sauerkraut (don't used canned), to yield 1/2–2/3 cup juice
2 cups sour cream
5 cups buttermilk

1/2 cup aquavit
2 teaspoons ground fennel seeds
3/4 pound medium shrimp
8–10 tablespoons minced dill
4 hard-boiled eggs (see page 39), sliced lengthwise
8 tablespoons salmon caviar

1. Peel, seed, and dice the cucumbers. Put in a colander and sprinkle with coarse salt. Let sit for 30 minutes.

2. Put the sauerkraut in a sieve over a bowl and press down hard with a wooden spoon to extract the juice. Save the sauerkraut for another use.

3. In a large bowl, combine the sour cream, buttermilk, aquavit, sauerkraut juice, and fennel seeds. Stir to combine.

4. Run the cucumbers under cold water, drain, and pat dry with paper towels. Add to the soup and chill for at least 8 hours.

5. In an uncovered saucepan, cook the shrimp in boiling salted water to cover for 3 minutes. Turn off the heat and let the shrimp cool in the liquid. Shell, devein, and cut into ½-inch pieces if the shrimp are large. Refrigerate until ready to serve.

6. Fill each chilled soup bowl with soup. Sprinkle with about 1 tablespoon of the minced dill. Place an egg slice in the center of each bowl, and arrange 3 or 4 shrimp slices around the egg. Top the egg with about 1 tablespoon of the caviar and serve immediately.

⫿

The New York Times reported on September 30, 1941, that the first thing Lord Beaverbrook did on his war-related mission in Moscow was to buy a gift for Prime Minister Winston Churchill: twenty-five pounds of caviar to be sent to Churchill by the quickest route. Beaverbrook bought himself a pot of strawberry jam.

PASTA, RICE, AND KASHA

The recipes in this chapter are suitable as both first courses and entrées.

Ludwig Bemelmans reported that "In Paris there was a great gourmet who had Cartier construct a little gold ball which he wore on the other end of his watch chain. He would go to one of the good restaurants, have his plate heaped with caviar and then drop the golden sphere from a foot above the plate. If it passed through the caviar without effort, he pronounced it first rate. If the ball got stuck in its passage and did not reach the bottom of the plate, he sent the plate and the black stuff back to the kitchen."

BOW TIES WITH RED AND BLACK CAVIAR, TOMATOES, AND BASIL

SERVES 4–6

2 pounds ripe tomatoes
1 pound bow ties (farfalle)
5 tablespoons olive oil
Salt
Freshly ground black pepper
2 tablespoons chopped fresh
  basil (don't substitute dried

basil; use fresh parsley if
fresh basil is unavailable)
¾ pound mozzarella, diced
6–8 tablespoons imported or
  domestic sturgeon caviar
6–8 tablespoons salmon
  caviar

1.   Peel the tomatoes by first plunging them into boiling water for 10 seconds. Remove with a slotted spoon and place in the sink. The tip of a sharp knife will slip easily between the skin and the flesh and from there the job of skinning is a snap. Remove the core and halve each tomato horizontally. Remove the seeds with the handle end of a spoon or with your thumb—the most efficient tool for the job. Salt each half lightly and turn cut side over on paper towels to drain for at least 15 minutes.

2.   Cook the pasta for about 10 minutes in a large quantity of lightly salted boiling water. Drain and toss with 4 tablespoons of the olive oil, salt, and pepper. Cool to room temperature.

3.   Dice the tomatoes. You should have about 3 cups.

4.   Toss the cooled pasta with the chopped basil and place on a 12-inch platter or in a shallow bowl. Pile the diced mozzarella in the center of the platter, over the pasta. Surround with the diced tomatoes. Dribble the last tablespoon of the olive oil over the cheese and tomatoes.

5.   Mound the sturgeon caviar on the cheese and scatter the salmon caviar over the outer ring of pasta. Serve immediately.

VODKA-CAVIAR PASTA

SERVES 6–8

1 pound angel-hair pasta
4 tablespoons (½ stick)
  unsalted butter, at room
  temperature
2 cups heavy cream
2 tablespoons vodka (pepper
  flavored, if you can find it)

2 egg yolks, at room
  temperature
8 tablespoons golden white-
  fish caviar

1.   Cook the pasta in a large quantity of boiling salted water for 5 or 6 minutes.
2.   Melt 1 tablespoon of the butter in a saucepan and add the cream and vodka. Simmer gently for a few minutes to reduce and thicken the cream.
3.   In the bowl in which you plan to serve the pasta, beat the egg yolks for a minute or two with the remaining 3 tablespoons butter. Add the drained pasta and the reduced cream. Gently stir in half the caviar, mounding the remainder on top. Serve immediately.

ANGEL-HAIR PASTA WITH CAVIAR

This is very simple, very delicious, and very expensive.

SERVES 6–8

1 pound angel-hair pasta
6 tablespoons unsalted butter
Salt

Freshly ground black pepper
6–8 tablespoons beluga or
  sevruga caviar

1.   Cook the pasta in a large quantity of boiling salted water for 5 or 6 minutes, or until al dente.

2.   Drain the pasta and place in a warm serving bowl with the butter. Toss and taste, adding salt and pepper as needed. Toss again, very gently, with the caviar, and serve immediately.

PASTA SHELLS
WITH SMOKED SALMON AND SALMON CAVIAR

This looks both beautiful and luxurious; it tastes wonderful. The entire dish is quick and simple to prepare and can be made several hours in advance of serving. You can save money without any loss of taste or quality by buying smoked salmon ends or trimmings. These result from the errors of amateur slicers (slicing salmon is a skill that takes time to master) as well as from the leftover ends from sides that have yielded the perfect paper-thin slices at four times the cost. You will have to do a little trimming of bone, cartilage, and fat, but it doesn't take long and the savings are worth the five minutes trimming will take you.

SERVES 6

*2 bunches arugula (about 8
    ounces, before removing
    stems)*
1 pound large pasta shells
7 tablespoons olive oil
3 tablespoons lemon juice
*7 scallions, including 2 to 3
    inches of green top,
    shredded*

1 tablespoon minced shallots
*½ pound smoked salmon,
    coarsely chopped*
*8–10 tablespoons salmon
    caviar*
1 lemon, cut into wedges

1.   Soak the arugula in several changes of cold water to remove all the sand, dirt, and grit. Remove stems and dry leaves thoroughly.

2. Cook the shells in a large quantity of boiling salted water for about 12 minutes; they should be al dente. Drain and toss with 4 tablespoons of the olive oil and 2 tablespoons of the lemon juice. Add the scallions, shallots, and smoked salmon. Combine well.

3. Put the arugula on a platter. Toss with the remaining 3 tablespoons olive oil and 1 tablespoon lemon juice.

4. Place the cooled pasta on the arugula. Just before serving, carefully spoon over the caviar. Serve garnished with lemon wedges.

HOW TO MAKE YOUR OWN SALMON CAVIAR

Should you be so lucky as to catch or receive a fresh female salmon from September on through spawning season, you might want to make your own salmon caviar. Freshness is all important: prepare the caviar within twenty-four hours of the fish being caught. A heavy, oily aroma is naturally present in the membrane, but do not use any roe with the odor of spoilage. What you are after is the fragile skein, a tenacious membrane that binds the multitude of eggs into a single unit. A 12- to 14-pound female salmon will contain on the average about a ½-pound skein, yielding 1 to 1½ cups of eggs, depending upon your dexterity, patience, and the maturity of the eggs.

You should try to get a mature skein so the membrane will come apart easily. Tight, stiff, tough membranes holding small eggs will be too difficult to work with. With a paring knife, make a slice from the back of the skein. Pick at the membrane with the knife to separate and remove the membrane. You will inevitably lose a few eggs, but if every egg breaks, discard the skein. If the skein is mature enough, you might be able to pop the eggs individually from the skein with your fingertips. However you do it, the more membrane you remove at this stage, the easier the task becomes later.

Wash the eggs in cold water. For 1 to 2 cups of cleaned eggs, make a brine of ½ cup salt to 2 cups cold water. Place in a large bowl and stir until the salt is mostly dissolved. Pour the eggs in and swirl about briefly. Let stand for 30 minutes to firm up and absorb some salt. The membrane particles will turn white and you should pluck them out. Pour the caviar into a wire strainer, draining off the salty water. Immerse the roe in a large bowl of cold water, swirling gently to rinse, then pour through a wire strainer again. Pick out all remaining membrane. Chill, covered, before serving. Keep tightly covered and refrigerated up to a few weeks, as long as the flavor is pleasant.

Kate Harris, who lives in Seattle, Washington, sometimes catches her own salmon. After removing the eggs from the membrane (she uses the knife method, finding it easier) and washing them in cold water, she puts them in a bowl of soy sauce, sometimes adding a little sake and a few slices of fresh ginger. Depending upon the saltiness of the brand of soy sauce, the roe can remain from 30 minutes to as long as overnight in the soy marinade. Drain and keep in a tightly covered jar in the refrigerator. These eggs, which will be an orange-brown color, not red, are delicious eaten with a spoon straight from the jar or on toast or fresh bread.

PASTA WITH RICOTTA AND CAVIAR

SERVES 4

½ pound spinach bow ties
(farfalle)
4 tablespoons (½ stick)
unsalted butter
4 tablespoons ricotta cheese

4 tablespoons heavy cream
Freshly ground black pepper
Salt
4 tablespoons salmon caviar

1. Cook the bow ties in a large quantity of rapidly boiling salted water for 8 to 10 minutes; the pasta should be al dente.
2. Melt the butter in a large skillet. Add the ricotta, cream, a generous amount of freshly ground black pepper, and a little salt. Stir over low heat for 2 minutes.
3. Drain the pasta and add to the skillet. Cook over low heat, stirring constantly, for 1 minute.
4. Transfer to a serving dish, add the caviar, toss, and serve.

CREAMY PASTA

This pasta should be served warm or tepid. You can make it about a half hour before you plan to serve. Don't refrigerate. This is a rich dish, more suitable as an appetizer than as an entrée.

SERVES 6–8

1 pound linguine
2 hard-boiled egg yolks (see
page 39)
4 tablespoons minced chives
or scallion tops
½ cup sour cream

1 cup heavy cream
1 teaspoon lemon juice
Salt
Freshly ground black pepper
6–8 tablespoons golden
whitefish caviar

1. Cook the pasta in a large quantity of boiling salted water for about 5 minutes; it should be al dente.
2. Sieve the yolks into the bowl in which you plan to serve. Add the chives. Drain the pasta and toss with the yolks and chives.
3. In a mixing bowl, combine the sour cream, heavy cream, and lemon juice. Beat for a moment, just to combine. Add to the pasta and toss with salt and pepper.
4. Just before serving, gently stir in 4 to 5 tablespoons of the caviar. Mound the remaining caviar on top. Serve on warm plates.

FUSILLI WITH SALMON CAVIAR AND FENNEL

Though I have varied it slightly, this recipe was created by Daniel Halpern and Julie Strand, who published it in their book, *The Good Food* (Viking Press, 1984).

SERVES 4–6

4 tablespoons grated Parmesan cheese
1 egg yolk
1 pound fusilli
2 tablespoons unsalted butter
1 cup heavy cream

¼ cup chopped fresh fennel leaves or dill
8–10 tablespoons salmon caviar
Freshly ground black pepper

1. In a small bowl, beat 1 tablespoon of the cheese with the egg yolk. Set aside.
2. Bring a large quantity of salted water to a boil and add the fusilli. Boil for about 8 minutes, until al dente. Drain well.
3. While the pasta is cooking, melt the butter in a small skillet. Add the cream and, stirring, cook about 5 minutes, until the cream is slightly thickened. Remove from the heat and stir a little of the

hot sauce into the egg-yolk-and-cheese mixture. Add the remaining Parmesan and the fennel or dill. Stir it all back into the hot cream. 4. Toss the pasta with the sauce in a warmed serving bowl. Add salmon caviar and freshly ground black pepper. Toss gently and serve immediately.

PENNE WITH TUNA AND BOTARGA

SERVES 4–6

1 cup chopped onion
2 teaspoons minced garlic
3 tablespoons olive oil
1 cup chopped canned
* tomatoes*
1 teaspoon dried orange peel
¼ teaspoon red pepper flakes
½ teaspoon dried basil, or
* 1 tablespoon minced fresh*
* basil*

One 6½-ounce can tuna,
* drained*
4 tablespoons (1 ounce)
* botarga*
1 pound penne
2 tablespoons lemon juice
¼ cup chopped parsley

1. In a skillet, sauté the onion and garlic over low heat in the olive oil until the onion softens, about 15 minutes. Add the tomatoes, orange peel, red pepper flakes, and dried basil (fresh goes in later). Cook, covered, for 15 minutes. Add the drained tuna and all but 1 tablespoon of the *botarga*. Stir and cook covered for 5 minutes more. 2. In a large quantity of boiling salted water, cook the penne for about 10 minutes; they should be al dente. Drain and add to the skillet along with the lemon juice, half the parsley, and the basil if you are using fresh. Toss for a moment over low heat. Sprinkle with remaining parsley and *botarga*. Serve immediately.

CAVIAR RISOTTO

Creamy and delicious, risotto is a satisfying first course; the addition of caviar makes it quite elegant.

SERVES 4

1 cup bottled clam juice
4 tablespoons (½ stick)
   unsalted butter
4–5 tablespoons minced onion
1½ cups long-grained or
   arborio rice

½ cup aquavit, dry ver-
   mouth, or dry white wine
1 cup heavy cream
6 tablespoons salmon caviar

1.   In a saucepan, mix the clam juice with 4 cups water and bring to a simmer.
2.   Melt the butter in a heavy saucepan and sauté the onion slowly in it, stirring from time to time. The onion should be soft but not browned.
3.   Add the rice and stir to coat with the butter and onion. Raise the heat and pour in the aquavit or wine. Boil off the alcohol, stirring constantly.
4.   Lower the heat, add 1 cup of the simmering liquid, and keep stirring until all the liquid is absorbed. Add another cup of simmering liquid, and stir until that's absorbed. Keep adding liquid until the rice is creamy but still firm. Toward the end of the cooking time, add the simmering liquid in smaller quantities; never stop stirring or the rice will stick and burn. After the last of the liquid has been absorbed and the rice is virtually done, add the heavy cream, stirring to combine. Turn off the heat and cover the pan with a folded dish towel. Let sit for 2 or 3 minutes. Gently stir in the caviar and serve immediately.

KASHA

In Russia, kasha is the word for all cereals. In the United States, it refers only to buckwheat groats, which are not technically a grain, but the edible fruit of the buckwheat plant. Kasha is widely available, sold packaged in supermarkets or loose in health-food stores. It has a rich nutty flavor, is simple to cook, reheats perfectly, and is a nutritional powerhouse. One serving provides a quarter of the recommended daily allowance of protein for the average adult. Buckwheat groats are also a good source of thiamin, niacin, riboflavin, potassium, and iron. Finally, it is good both hot and cold.

SERVES 4–6

1 large egg
*1 cup whole roasted buck-
    wheat groats (do not buy
    medium or fine kasha)*
Salt
*2 cups homemade or canned
    chicken stock or water*

*2 tablespoons rendered
    chicken fat or unsalted
    butter*
1 cup sour cream
6 tablespoons salmon caviar

1. Beat the egg in a small bowl just to combine the white and yolk. Stir in the kasha and a pinch of salt. Canned chicken stock will be saltier than homemade; if you use water, as much as ½ teaspoon salt might be necessary. Stir until thoroughly combined.
2. Put the kasha in a medium-size, heavy ungreased frying pan—cast iron is best. Toast the groats over moderate heat until the grains separate and give off a nutty smell. Stir frequently from the bottom with a wooden spoon as they are likely to stick. Be careful not to burn the groats.
3. In a 2-quart heavy saucepan with a lid, bring the chicken stock or water to a boil. Slowly, stir in the toasted groats. Add the chicken fat or butter, cover the saucepan tightly (to trap the steam), and cook over the lowest possible heat until all the liquid is absorbed,

15 to 20 minutes. The kasha can also be cooked, for the same amount of time, in a 325-degree F. oven. The grains should be dry and separate. You can fluff with a fork and serve immediately, or if you have the time or want the kasha to wait, cover it with a folded dish towel, replace the lid, and keep in a 250-degree F. oven for as long as you like. The kasha will improve.

4.   Serve with sour cream and caviar.

NOTE: To reheat, you can steam in a colander or steamer over boiling water, covered with a dish towel. Or, you can turn the kasha into a buttered casserole and heat through in a 350-degree F. oven.

ENTRÉES

As the focus of a meal, these recipes are all dazzling; and, on the whole, they are quick and simple to prepare.

ıllı

"Charles Chaplin has sold a 1,000-word excerpt from his autobiography to the Soviet newspaper *Izvestia* for nine pounds of caviar, his publishers said today.
"*Izvestia* could have published as much as it wanted without asking permission because the Soviet Union is not a member of the International Coypright Convention. But it asked permission 'because of the great respect with which Mr. Chaplin is held in Russia,' a spokesman for the publishers, Bodley Head, Ltd., said.
"Alexei Adzhubei, editor of *Izvestia*, became interested in the autobiography after reading the first installment in a London newspaper. The Chaplins are fond of caviar, the spokesman said."

The New York Times, September 22, 1964

BLINIS

In prerevolutionary Russia, blinis were served during *maslenitsa*, the "butterweek" festival celebrated the week before Lent, much like Mardi Gras. Throughout the day, street vendors sold hot blinis so fast they didn't have time to cool: stacks and stacks were consumed, served with melted butter, sour cream, caviar, herring, smoked sturgeon, salmon, and whitefish, all accompanied by chilled, often flavored, vodka.

In Russia, blinis were originally made with buckwheat flour, which is indigenous to that country. It is also the typical folkloric flour of Brittany, in France, where the original crêpes were made of it. In France, buckwheat flour is known as *gruau de sarrasin*, oddly honoring the invaders who introduced the native central Asian grain there. In both Brittany and Russia—damp, windy, cold, generally inhospitable agricultural climates—buckwheat would grow where more refined wheat wouldn't. White flour is produced in the United States and Canada in such abundance that the entire world can be supplied; that richness, coupled with modern, sophisticated grain supply routes, obliterated the need to grow the less versatile and useful buckwheat.

Buckwheat blinis are heartier, firmer, and darker in color than white flour blinis. Recipes for three types of blinis follow: those that use buckwheat flour alone, buckwheat and white flour, and white flour alone. Both yeast and baking powder batters are offered. Yeast is great fun to work with: its properties seem magical. Yet it gives no detectable physical clues to its rising abilities; and indeed, not every package will produce the magic. So don't fail to prove the yeast before using it. It should increase considerably in bulk, have a bubbly surface, and look spongey.

No matter which batter you use, the blinis should be about 5 inches in diameter, thicker than a crêpe, but thinner than an American breakfast pancake. Ideally they should be made one at a time in a 4-to-6-inch cast-iron skillet or iron crêpe pan, well seasoned so the blini won't stick to the pan. Blinis can also be cooked on a very hot griddle, several at a time.

To keep the blinis hot while cooking the rest, either put them on a cookie sheet in a 200-degree F. oven, or create a bain marie by putting a large bowl in a large pan of very hot water. Serve as soon as they are all done.

A festive way to serve blinis, as the central dish of a dinner, is to pass them with bowls of sour cream, melted clarified butter (see page 41), and an assortment of caviars. Each diner then serves himself. In Russia, the blinis are eaten with melted butter and caviar, not melted butter, caviar, and sour cream. There, the sour cream is eaten alone on a blini, as a kind of palate cleanser, midway through the feast. Authentic or not, a really sublime combination is a blini served with melted butter, crème fraîche, and pressed caviar. Crème fraîche or sour cream is also good with salmon caviar and blinis. Minced red onion, scallions, or shallots are very good sprinkled on a sour cream blini, and a small bowl should be included among your filling offerings, as should lemon halves, wrapped tightly in cheese-cloth (to prevent pits from falling onto the blini).

Another splendid combination is to interleave three or four 3- or 4-inch buckwheat blinis per serving with sliced goat cheese, melted butter poured over, and topped with a tablespoon or so of golden whitefish caviar.

It is impossible to specify the quantity of blinis, caviar, sour cream or crème fraîche, and melted butter you will need. As an entrée, you can roughly calculate that each diner will eat about five or six blinis, perhaps two or three as an appetizer. For six people you should provide about 1 cup sour cream or crème fraîche, 1 cup (2 sticks) warm unsalted clarified butter, and perhaps 10 ounces of caviar. Each blini will comfortably hold about 2 teaspoons butter, and/or 1 tablespoon sour cream, and about 2 teaspoons caviar.

"I was there twenty minutes before Rex. If I had to spend an evening with him, it should, at any rate, be in my own way. I remember the dinner well—soup of *oseille*, a sole quite simply cooked in a white wine sauce, a *caneton à la presse*, a lemon soufflé. At the last minute, fearing that the whole thing was too simple for Rex, I added *caviare aux blinis.* . . . The cream and hot butter mingled and overflowed separating each glaucose bead of caviar from its fellows, capping it in white and gold.

" 'I like a bit of chopped onion with mine,' Rex said. 'Chap-who-knew told me it brought out the flavor.'

" 'Try it without first,' I said."

EVELYN WAUGH,
Brideshead Revisited (Little, Brown, 1945)

A FEW TIPS ON MAKING BLINIS

1) Keep a small saucepan of clarified butter (see page 41) over very low heat and pour from that into the skillets. Depending on the type of skillet, you may need to put additional butter in after each pancake (enamel) or every third pancake (cast iron).

2) Regulate the heat so the blinis don't burn, taking a pan out of service for a few minutes if it gets too hot.

3) The easiest way to make the blinis is to pour in the butter and the batter off the heat and rotate the pan before putting it over moderate heat.

4) The finished blini will keep warm for about an hour in a small pot nestled in a larger pot filled with hot water. Turn the heat on periodically to keep the water hot. Make sure it doesn't boil over into the pan with the blinis. Keep the blinis covered with aluminum foil.

5) It will take about 30 minutes of frying (and paying attention every one of those minutes) to make a batch of blinis. It is a laborious business.

6) If you have blinis leftover, wrap them tightly in plastic wrap *and* aluminum foil and freeze. To use, place the foil-wrapped package, frozen, on a steamer over an inch or so of boiling water. Put the cover on the pot and steam for about 10 minutes, until the blinis are hot.

BUCKWHEAT BLINIS

MAKES 18-20

One ¼-ounce package dry
    active yeast
1 teaspoon sugar
1 teaspoon salt
2 cups buckwheat flour
1 cup lukewarm (90–100
    degrees F.) water
1 cup scalded milk, cooled to
    lukewarm (90–100
    degrees F.)

3 eggs, at room temperature,
    separated
2 tablespoons unsalted butter,
    melted and cooled
6–8 tablespoons clarified
    butter, for frying (see page
    41)

1. In a small bowl, combine the yeast, ½ teaspoon of the sugar, and 2 tablespoons lukewarm water (100 degrees F.). Stir to combine and set aside for 10 minutes. The yeast should increase substantially in bulk and look bubbly.

2. In a large bowl, combine the remaining ½ teaspoon sugar, the salt, and buckwheat flour. Slowly stir in the liquids to form a smooth batter. Add the lightly beaten egg yolks and the yeast mixture. Stir again, cover with a dish towel, and set aside to rise, about 1 hour.

3. When the batter has risen to twice its original volume, beat the egg whites with a pinch of salt until soft peaks form. Stir in the melted butter. Gently fold in the egg whites. Cover and let rise again until double in bulk. This rising should take 30 to 45 minutes in a warm kitchen.

4. Heat some clarified butter in one or two 5-inch skillets. Dip a ¼-cup measure into the batter and pour into the hot buttered pan. Immediately rotate the pan to cover the bottom evenly with batter. In about 1 minute, the surface of the blini will be covered with bubbles and the bottom should be golden. Turn and fry the other side until golden. Remove to a bain marie or keep in a 200-degree F. oven, and continue frying.

BUCKWHEAT AND WHITE FLOUR BLINIS

MAKES 24

One ¼-ounce package dry
  active yeast
1½ teaspoons sugar
3 cups milk, scalded and
  cooled to room temperature
1 cup buckwheat flour
1 cup unbleached white flour

½ teaspoon salt
3 eggs, separated
2 tablespoons unsalted butter,
  melted and cooled
8 tablespoons clarified butter,
  for frying (see page 41)

1.   In a small bowl, combine the yeast, ½ teaspoon of the sugar, and 2 tablespoons lukewarm (100 degrees F.) water. Set aside for 10 minutes. The yeast should increase substantially in bulk and look bubbly. If it doesn't, start again with fresh yeast.

2.   In a large bowl, mix together ½ cup of the buckwheat flour, ½ cup of the unbleached flour, the remaining 1 teaspoon sugar, and the salt. Make a well in the center and add the egg yolks, lightly beaten, the cooled milk, and the yeast. Stirring with a wooden spoon, combine the wet and dry ingredients. Cover with a dish towel and let rise until double in bulk, about 1 hour.

3.   Mix the remaining ½ cups of flour. When the batter is doubled, add the flours alternately with the melted butter. Mix with a wooden spoon to form a smooth batter. Cover and let double in bulk again. This will take another hour in a warm kitchen or 4 or 5 hours in a cool room.

4.   Just before making the blinis, beat the egg whites with a pinch of salt until soft peaks form. Gently fold them into the batter.

5.   Heat some clarified butter in one or two or (if you can manage it) three 5-inch crêpe pans, cast-iron skillets, or enamel frying pans. Dip a ¼-cup measure into the batter and pour into the hot buttered pan. Immediately rotate the pan to cover the bottom evenly with the batter. A ¼ cup of batter in a 5-inch skillet should yield a blini of perfect thickness and size. In a minute or so, tiny bubbles will appear

on the top of the blini and the edges will be set. Turn and cook on the second side for another minute. Remove to a bain marie or a 200-degree F. oven and continue frying.

WHITE FLOUR BLINIS

These blinis are richer, lighter, and more delicate than those made with buckwheat flour.

MAKES 30

One ¼-ounce package dry
  active yeast
2 teaspoons sugar
4½ cups unbleached flour
2½ cups warm (105 degrees
  F.) milk
2 eggs, separated

Salt
4 tablespoons (½ stick)
  unsalted butter, melted and
  cooled
1 cup heavy cream, whipped
8 tablespoons clarified butter,
  for frying (see page 41)

1.   In a small bowl, combine the yeast, ½ teaspoon of the sugar, and 2 tablespoons lukewarm (100 degrees F.) water. Stir and set aside for 10 minutes. The yeast should increase substantially in bulk and look bubbly.
2.   In a large bowl, combine 3½ cups of the flour, the milk, egg yolks, lightly beaten, 1 teaspoon salt, and the remaining 1½ teaspoons sugar. Stir to combine and add the yeast mixture. Beat for 3 or 4 minutes with a wooden spoon or for 1 minute in a standing electric mixer. Cover with a dish towel and set aside in a warm place to rise until double in bulk, about 1 hour.
3.   When the batter is doubled, add the remaining 1 cup flour, the melted butter, and the whipped cream. Beat with a wooden spoon for 5 or 6 minutes; or 3 or 4 minutes in a standing electric mixer. Cover and let rise again until double in bulk. This will take about 30 to 45 minutes in a warm place.

4. Just before you are ready to fry the blinis, beat the egg whites with a pinch of salt until soft peaks form. Gently fold into the batter.
5. Heat some clarified butter in one or more 5-inch skillets. Fill a ¼-cup measure with batter and pour into the hot buttered pan. Rotate the pan to spread the batter evenly and place over moderate heat. In a minute or so, the bottom will be golden. Turn and fry the other side for another minute, or less. Remove to a bain marie or low oven (200 degrees F.) to keep warm while you finish making the blinis.

QUICK BLINIS

If you have a craving for blinis and don't want to wait two hours for yeast batter to rise, these are more than respectable. They are delicious and are made in a matter of minutes.

MAKES 24

4 eggs, separated	*3 cups buttermilk, or 2 cups*
1 tablespoon sugar	*whole milk and 1 cup sour*
3 cups unbleached flour	*cream*
1 teaspoon salt	*2 teaspoons double-acting*
8 tablespoons (1 stick)	*baking powder*
unsalted butter, melted and	*8 tablespoons clarified butter,*
cooled	*for frying (see page 41)*

1. Put the yolks and the sugar in the bowl of a standing electric mixer and beat for 2 or 3 minutes at medium speed. Add the flour, salt, melted butter, and buttermilk or whole milk and sour cream. Beat for 2 minutes more at moderate speed.
2. Add the baking powder and mix thoroughly.
3. In another bowl beat the egg whites with a pinch of salt until soft peaks form. Gently fold the whites into the batter.

4.   Heat some of the clarified butter in a cast-iron skillet or a crêpe pan or a griddle. Fill a ¼-cup measure with the batter, pour into the pan, and rotate to spread the batter evenly. The blinis should cook in about 90 seconds: 60 seconds on the first side and 30 seconds on the reverse. Stack and keep warm in a low oven (200 degrees F.) or in a bain marie until all are fried and ready to serve.

WHOLE POACHED SALMON

A whole poached salmon is a glorious, luxurious, and tempting sight on a buffet table. It is easy to prepare and impressive to serve. The only trick is finding something long enough in which to poach it. A 10-pound salmon will measure around 30 inches from nose to tail. A fish poacher with a removable rack is perfect. If you don't have one, use a turkey roaster. You can cut off the head and/or the tail if your pot requires; use your decorative ability to disguise the disfigurement when you serve. Count on ½ to ¾ pound clean, raw salmon per person.

1 salmon, 5–10 pounds
2 teaspoons salt
1½ cups chopped carrots
1½ cups chopped celery, including some leaves
2 cups sliced leek greens
1 teaspoon dried thyme
2 teaspoons black peppercorns
White wine vinegar
Parsley sprigs
8–10 tablespoons salmon caviar

Sour Cream–Caviar Mayonnaise (see page 111)
Cucumber–Sour Cream Sauce (see page 119)
Cucumber-Caviar Sauce (see page 111)
Russian Dressing (without the beets, page 141)
Caviar Beurre Blanc (see page 120)

1. Have the fish cleaned but not scaled. Have fins left on, and if you want to cook and serve the salmon with its head on, remove the gills. Wrap the fish in several layers of washed cheesecloth or a dish towel so it will keep its shape during the cooking. Tie lightly in a few places with string. If you are poaching in a roaster, lay the fish on a double length of aluminum foil which can later be used as handles to remove the fish from the liquid. If you have cut off the head, place it in the poacher beside the rest of the fish.

2. Put the salt, carrots, celery, leeks, thyme, and black peppercorns in a saucepan with 3 quarts cold water. Bring to a simmer and cook covered for 15 minutes. Let the stock cool to room temperature. Pour the unstrained stock into the fish poacher or roaster or whatever you have chosen for poaching. Lower the rack or foil holder into the liquid. Measuring, add enough cold water to cover. Counting the 3 quarts of water used in the stock, and water poured in to cover the fish, add 1½ tablespoons white wine vinegar for each 2 quarts of water.

3. Put the fish poacher across two burners, and don't cover the poacher with the lid or the liquid might overheat, causing the salmon to twist and break. Bring the liquid to a low simmer—185 degrees F. on a thermometer. A 7-pound salmon will take 20 minutes, a 10-pound salmon, 30 minutes. Turn off the heat and let the salmon rest in the hot liquid for at least 30 minutes, or up to 2 hours if you are serving it hot or warm. If you plan to serve the salmon cold, leave for several hours to cool completely in the liquid.

4. Remove the salmon from the liquid and place on a platter. Cut the string and gently remove the cheesecloth or towel, drawing it out from under the fish. With a sharp knife and your fingers, remove fins and any small protruding bones. Peel off the skin with a knife and your fingers. The soft brown flesh on top of the salmon will scrape off easily—don't dig or press hard—to reveal the pink flesh beneath.

5. Place parsley all around the salmon and scatter the caviar over the fish and the parsley. If the head was detached, put it in place and camouflage with parsley.

6.   To serve the salmon, run a thin, sharp knife along the middle of the salmon, down to the central bone. Remove portions from the top, then remove the backbone, and serve from the bottom half.

7.   Serve the salmon, warm or cool, with Sour Cream–Caviar Mayonnaise or one or more of the sauces listed.

Sour Cream–Caviar Mayonnaise

1 cup mayonnaise	*4 tablespoons sour cream*
2 teaspoons lemon juice	*4 tablespoons salmon caviar*
2 tablespoons minced dill	

1.   If you are using commercial mayonnaise, add the lemon juice; if your mayonnaise is homemade, it probably won't need it. Combine with the remaining ingredients, gently adding the caviar just before serving.

BROILED SWORDFISH
WITH CUCUMBER-CAVIAR SAUCE

The contrast between the hot fish and the cold sauce is very pleasing. This dish can be made in 20 minutes, from start to finish. If you make the sauce in advance, don't put the cucumbers in until the last minute: the water they exude will dilute the sauce.

SERVES 6

3 pounds swordfish, 1 inch thick	*3 tablespoons unsalted butter*
	Salt
1 tablespoon vegetable oil	*Freshly ground black pepper*

Cucumber-Caviar Sauce

1 cup peeled, seeded, and diced cucumber	*1 tablespoon minced chives or parsley*
1 ½ cups sour cream	*4 tablespoons salmon caviar*
1 tablespoon grated onion	

1. Preheat the broiler.
2. Brush the hot broiler rack with the vegetable oil, and the fish with a pat of the butter, some salt, and freshly ground black pepper.
3. Broil the fish about 3 inches from the heat. After 5 minutes, brush the fish with another pat of the butter and broil for 2 minutes more.
4. Carefully turn the fish and brush with more butter; sprinkle with salt and more pepper. Broil for 5 minutes, brush with more butter, and broil for 2 to 3 additional minutes.
5. While the fish is broiling, make the sauce by combining the cucumbers, sour cream, onion, minced herbs, and, immediately before serving, the caviar.

BRAISED VEAL WITH CAVIAR SAUCE

This dish is easy to prepare and its creamy piquancy makes it very good to eat.

SERVES 8

One 4-pound shoulder veal
  roast, tied
Salt
Freshly ground black pepper
2 tablespoons unsalted butter
1 cup chopped onion
½ cup chopped carrots
½ cup chopped celery
1 bay leaf

6 whole black peppercorns
4 parsley sprigs
1 cup dry white wine
1 cup chicken stock
½ cup heavy cream
2 teaspoons lemon juice
1 teaspoon grated lemon zest
4 tablespoons imported or
  domestic sturgeon caviar

1. Dry the meat with paper towels and rub with salt and pepper.

2. In a heavy skillet, brown the meat on all sides in the butter.

3. In a large, heavy pot (with a lid) that will comfortably hold all the ingredients, put the vegetables, bay leaf, peppercorns, parsley, wine, and stock. Bring to a boil, add the meat, lower the heat, cover, and braise for 1½ to 2 hours, until the meat is tender.

4. Remove the meat and cover loosely with foil. Strain the sauce through a sieve into a bowl, pressing down on the vegetables with the back of a wooden spoon to get all the liquid out and to purée some of the vegetables to give more body to the sauce. Put the liquid back in the braising pot and boil for a few minutes to reduce and intensify the flavor. Add the heavy cream and bring to the boil. Off the heat, at the last moment, add the lemon juice, zest, and caviar.

5. Slice the meat and place on a platter. Spoon some of the sauce over the meat and pass the rest of the sauce separately.

FILLET OF SOLE STUFFED WITH CAVIAR AND WRAPPED IN SWISS CHARD

This looks terrific and is quick and simple to prepare. Spinach is a good substitute if you cannot find Swiss chard.

SERVES 6

6 *lemon or gray sole fillets, about 6 ounces each*	*3–4 tablespoons golden whitefish caviar*
Salt	*8–10 large Swiss chard leaves,*
Freshly ground black pepper	*trimmed of central rib but*
3 tablespoons unsalted butter, at room temperature	*left whole*
	Lemon wedges

1. Season the fillets lightly with salt and pepper. Place on the rack of a fish poacher or on a steamer in a large pot with about an inch of simmering water. Fold the fillets in half if they won't fit on the

steamer. Put the cover on and steam for about 5 minutes, until the fish is opaque, but not quite done.

2.   Remove the rack or steamer with the fillets on it. Keep the water in the pot at a simmer. When the fillets are cool enough to handle, put ½ tablespoon of the butter and ½ tablespoon of the caviar in the center of each. Roll and place each fillet on a chard leaf. Fold and wrap as neatly as you can, making sure to enclose the fish completely. Patch with additional pieces of chard and secure with toothpicks, if necessary.

3.   Put the fillets back on the rack of the poacher or on the steamer. Cover and cook for 2 to 3 minutes. Serve immediately, garnished with lemon wedges.

BLINTZES

These cheese-filled crêpes are delicious with caviar.

SERVES 6

2 eggs	1 cup milk
1 tablespoon unsalted butter, melted and cooled	¼ teaspoon double-acting baking powder
1 cup unbleached flour	4 tablespoons (½ stick)
½ teaspoon salt	unsalted butter

Filling

½ pound farmer or pot cheese	Salt
2 ounces (4 tablespoons) cream cheese, at room temperature	½ tablespoon grated lemon zest
	6 tablespoons salmon caviar
1 egg	1 cup sour cream

1.   To make the crêpes, lightly beat the eggs in a bowl. Add the melted butter, flour, salt, and milk. Stir until smooth. Add the baking powder.

2.   Melt a teaspoon or so of the butter in a 5- to 6-inch cast-iron skillet or other nonstick pan of the same diameter. When it's hot, add 2 tablespoons of the batter and immediately rotate the pan to spread the batter evenly and thinly over the bottom. Pour any excess back into the bowl. Cook for about 30 seconds on the first side. Slide the crêpe—you will have about a dozen—onto a small plate and flip it back into the pan. Cook for about 15 seconds more. As they are done, remove the crêpes to a cookie sheet. Add more butter to the pan as necessary. The cooked crêpes will keep for several hours at room temperature.

3.   To make the filling, combine the farmer or pot cheese, the cream cheese, egg, a pinch of salt, and the lemon zest. Beat with a wooden spoon until smooth, pressing through a sieve if the filling is lumpy. Finally, gently add 3 tablespoons of the caviar.

4.   To make the blintzes, put about 1 tablespoon of the filling in the center of each crêpe. Roll and fold so the filling is completely enclosed. Cook in a large frying pan in which you've heated more butter. Fry each for about 3 or 4 minutes, turning to brown all sides. Serve as soon as done, with sour cream and the remaining caviar.

SCALLOPS WITH CAVIAR

This dish is delicious served on a bed of steamed spinach.

SERVES 4

1½ pounds sea scallops
3 tablespoons unsalted butter
½ cup minced shallots
¾ cup dry white wine or
    white vermouth
¾ cup heavy cream

2 pounds spinach, steamed
4–5 tablespoons domestic
    sturgeon caviar, or golden
    whitefish caviar, or a
    combination of the two

1.   Slice large scallops in half, against the grain.
2.   Melt the butter in a heavy 10-inch skillet and add the shallots.

Cook slowly for 2 or 3 minutes. Add the wine and boil for 2 or 3 minutes, stirring as you do. Lower the heat and add the cream. Simmer for about 10 minutes, or until the sauce lightly coats a spoon. Add the scallops and cook for 2 minutes, just until the scallops turn opaque.

3. Transfer to a serving dish lined with steamed spinach. Place dollops of caviar on the scallops, alternating colors if you are using two kinds.

HALIBUT WITH CAVIAR-CREAM SAUCE

This dish originated in Astrakhan, the great caviar processing center at the head of the Volga delta. In Astrakhan this dish is made with Caspian beluga, sevruga, or osetra caviar. You might make it with one of those, or American sturgeon caviar, or with rinsed and drained black lumpfish caviar (see page 34).

SERVES 6

1 cup minced onion
1 cup minced celery
1 cup minced carrots
8 tablespoons (1 stick)
  unsalted butter
½ cup chopped parsley
3 bay leaves
2 whole cloves
Salt
Freshly ground black pepper
1 cup dry white wine

6 halibut steaks, about 6
  ounces each and ¾ inch
  thick
½ cup unbleached flour
½ cup heavy cream
2 teaspoons lemon juice
4 tablespoons caviar
1 hard-boiled egg, sieved
  (see page 39)
2 tablespoons minced chives

1. Sauté the vegetables in 4 tablespoons of the butter for about 10 minutes, until they are soft. Add the parsley, bay leaves, cloves, salt, and pepper. Cook covered over low heat for 15 minutes.

2. Add ½ cup of the white wine and simmer, uncovered, for 5 minutes.

3. Remove the bay leaves and purée the mixture in a food processor or pass through a food mill into a bowl. This will give body to the sauce without using a thickening agent.

4. Sprinkle the halibut with salt and pepper. Put the flour on a plate and dredge the fish in it, shaking off excess.

5. In a large, heavy sauté pan, sauté the fish in the remaining 4 tablespoons butter, in batches if necessary so as not to crowd the pan. Three minutes on each side should be enough; the fish should be golden. Transfer the fish to a platter and keep warm in a 200-degree F. oven.

6. Pour out the butter in which you sautéed the fish, and add the remaining ½ cup wine. Bring to a boil, scraping the bottom of the pan, and reduce the wine by half.

7. To the sauté pan, add the puréed vegetables and the heavy cream. Simmer, stirring, for a minute or two. Add the lemon juice. Remove from the heat and stir in 2 tablespoons of the caviar.

8. Pour the sauce over the fish and top each steak with 1 teaspoon of the caviar. Sprinkle with the sieved egg and minced chives and serve immediately.

BAKED HAKE WITH CAVIAR BUTTER

Hake is a delicious, inexpensive, firm-fleshed white fish. It is widely used and expertly cooked in Spain and Portugal where it is known as merluza.

SERVES 6

3 pounds hake fillet, 1 inch thick at the wider end
2 tablespoons unsalted butter

1 teaspoon lemon juice
4 tablespoons chopped parsley
Lemon wedges

Caviar Butter

6 tablespoons unsalted butter, at room temperature

4 tablespoons salmon caviar

1. Preheat the oven to 375 degrees F.
2. Put 1 tablespoon of the butter in a baking dish and place in the oven to melt.
3. Lay the fish in the melted butter and top with the remaining tablespoon butter. Sprinkle with lemon juice and cook for 20 to 25 minutes.
4. While the fish is baking, make the Caviar Butter by mashing the butter in a bowl until perfectly soft. Gently stir in the caviar. Refrigerate until ready to use.
5. To serve, transfer the fish to a platter and sprinkle with parsley. Spread the Caviar Butter down the center of the fish, so each serving will have some when the fish is cut into portions. Serve garnished with lemon wedges.

SALMON CROQUETTES

These are quick and easy to prepare and delicious to eat. One is plenty as an appetizer; two will be a hearty lunch or supper dish, served with bread and salad.

SERVES 4–6

1 pound cooked salmon
¾ cup fresh bread crumbs
2 eggs
¼ teaspoon cayenne
1 teaspoon Dijon mustard
2 teaspoons lemon juice
Salt

Freshly ground black pepper
2 tablespoons salmon caviar
¼ cup unbleached flour
½ teaspoon ground ginger
Vegetable oil and butter, for
*   frying*

Cucumber–Sour Cream Sauce

1 large cucumber
2 teaspoons coarse salt
1 cup sour cream

3 tablespoons heavy cream,
*   whipped*
3 tablespoons salmon caviar

1.   Flake the salmon into a bowl. Add the bread crumbs, eggs, cayenne, mustard, lemon juice, a little salt, and freshly ground black pepper. Mash and combine with a fork. Taste for seasoning.

2.   With your hands, form the mixture into ovals, about 3 inches long, 2 inches wide, and 1 inch high. Holding the croquette in the palm of your hand, make a wide slit in it with the edge of a spoon. Fill the depression with ¼ teaspoon of the caviar and re-form the croquette so the caviar is completely enclosed.

3.   On a large plate, combine the flour and ginger. Roll each croquette in the seasoned flour and place on a cookie sheet. When all the croquettes are lightly covered with the flour, place the cookie sheet in the refrigerator for at least an hour.

4.   When you are ready to cook, heat an equal quantity of oil and butter in a large, heavy skillet to reach a depth of ½ inch. Fry the croquettes for about 5 minutes, rolling them with chopsticks or

wooden spoons so all sides brown. Drain on paper towels for a moment and serve with the sauce.

5. To make the sauce, peel, seed, and dice the cucumber. Sprinkle with the salt and drain in a colander for about 15 minutes. Rinse and dry with paper towels. Combine with the sour cream, whipped cream, and 2 tablespoons of the caviar. Garnish the top of the sauce with the remaining tablespoon caviar. The sauce should be assembled just before serving.

STEAMED SCROD FILLETS
WITH CAVIAR BEURRE BLANC

Scrod is a small cod and is said to have been named by the Parker House, a famous old hotel and restaurant in Boston. The restaurant always offered the freshest fish of the day on its menu, but the manager never knew which this would be on a given day. So he invented the word scrod as a catchall. Although scrod now officially means young cod, it is historically correct to use for young haddock, too.

This dish can be made in 10 minutes from start to finish, and any white-fleshed fillets can be used.

SERVES 4

4 scrod, red snapper, flounder, or other firm, white-fleshed fillets, 6 ounces each
Salt
Freshly ground black pepper

Cayenne
2 tablespoons minced parsley
4 tablespoons minced red onion

Caviar Beurre Blanc

½ cup dry white wine
2 tablespoons minced shallots

6 tablespoons unsalted butter, chilled
2 tablespoons salmon caviar

1. Preheat the oven to 450 degrees F.
2. Cut four pieces of aluminum foil, each about 15 inches long. Butter the foil and lay a fillet on each. Sprinkle with salt, pepper, a pinch of cayenne (to remove any iodine flavor), ½ tablespoon of the minced parsley, and 1 tablespoon of the minced red onion on each. Bring the corners of the foil to the center and crimp the edges. The foil should completely enclose the fish, but not tightly. Place on a cookie sheet in the preheated oven. Half-inch-thick scrod will take about 7 minutes to cook; thinner fillets, such as red snapper, will take 4 or 5 minutes.
3. While the fish is baking, make the sauce. In a small saucepan over high heat, reduce the wine and shallots to about 3 tablespoons. Off the heat, beat in the butter, a small piece at a time. Finally, add the caviar. Serve each diner a foil package and pass the sauce separately.

POTATO PANCAKES

Latkes have traditionally been served among Jews at Chanukah. A special December treat, they seemed illicit at other times of the year. But latkes are too good to restrict to one week a year, and they are appearing with great frequency on restaurant menus and passed with drinks at cocktail parties, served with caviar and crème fraîche or sour cream.

It is impossible to say how many people will be served by a given quantity of potato pancakes. The yield for the recipe below is about forty 3- to 4-inch pancakes; six people would be amply served if you are offering only, say, soup and salad with them; eight to ten might be satisfied with them as a first course or an accompaniment to pot roast, as they always are at my mother's home at Chanukah. If you serve small, silver-dollar-size pancakes, the quantity below would yield about eighty pancakes. My experience is that no matter how many you make, no matter how few people are eating them, there are never leftovers.

6 large Idaho potatoes, 8–9 ounces each
3 medium onions
4 eggs
¼–½ cup unbleached flour
2–3 teaspoons salt
Freshly ground black pepper

Vegetable or peanut oil, for frying
Caviar: golden whitefish, salmon, and/or North American sturgeon
Sour cream or crème fraîche (see page 31)

1.   Peel the potatoes. If you are grating them by hand, use a large-holed grater. To grate in a food processor, dice the potatoes and process with the steel blade using several quick on-off motions. Texture is crucial and you don't want a purée nor do you want chunks. With each potato, process half an onion. As it is done, transfer each batch to a sieve placed over a bowl. Press out the moisture with the back of a wooden spoon and transfer the grated potatoes to another bowl. When all the potatoes and onions have been drained, discard the liquid in the bowl, but scrape the potato starch remaining on the bottom of the bowl into the grated potatoes and onions.

2.   In a small bowl, beat the eggs for a moment to combine the whites and yolks. Add to the grated potatoes. Shake in just enough flour to make a batter. Add the salt and plenty of freshly ground black pepper. The batter can be made several hours in advance of frying. Sprinkle flour over the top. The potatoes will darken somewhat, which won't matter after the pancakes are made. Some liquid will accumulate and should be poured off before frying.

3.   To fry the pancakes, heat enough oil to reach a depth of about ¼ inch in a large, heavy skillet. Drop about 2 tablespoons of the batter into the hot oil and flatten a bit with the back of a wooden spoon. If you want small cocktail pancakes, reduce the amount of batter you use for each pancake. If you want really flat pancakes, which will not have a soft interior, flatten the batter even thinner. The pancakes should cook about 2 minutes on the first side, and 30

seconds or so on the second. Leave plenty of room around each pancake in the pan—don't crowd. As each batch is finished, drain on paper towels and keep warm in a very low oven (200 degrees F.). The pancakes should be served as soon after cooking as possible as they lose their crispness as they wait. Reheated pancakes are not very interesting.

4. To serve the pancakes, either put a large platter of them in the middle of the table and pass the sour cream and the caviar (an assortment or one kind only) for each diner to serve himself; or put 4 pancakes (this is just a start) on a plate with 3 or 4 tablespoons of sour cream and 1 teaspoon (or so) of each of three different kinds of caviar or 1 tablespoon of a single caviar. If you are serving them at a cocktail party, put a teaspoon or so of sour cream on each pancake and top with a dollop of caviar. Iced vodka is the perfect accompaniment.

Variation: Add 2 tablespoons finely grated ginger to the batter. It's not traditional, but it's very tasty.

Egg Dishes

SMOKED SALMON FRITTATA

This is a beautiful dish, lovely to serve for lunch or supper. It's also good as an appetizer, sliced into thin wedges. Serve warm or at room temperature.

SERVES 4–6

6 eggs
Freshly ground black pepper
2 tablespoons minced chives
  or scallion tops
1 tablespoon olive oil

2 heaping tablespoons diced
  smoked salmon (about
  2 ounces)
½–¾ cup sour cream
4 tablespoons salmon caviar

1. Preheat the oven to 400 degrees F.
2. Break the eggs into a small bowl. Add freshly ground black pepper and the chives or scallion tops. Beat with a fork for a moment, just to combine the whites and yolks.
3. Heat the olive oil in a 6- to 8-inch cast-iron skillet or round cake pan. Add half the eggs, and cook as for an omelette, lifting the edges and rotating the pan for the uncooked eggs to flow underneath. When the eggs are just set, remove from the heat. Spread the smoked salmon in an even layer over the set eggs and pour on the uncooked eggs. Place in the preheated oven and cook for about 10 minutes, until the frittata is completely set and coming away from the sides of the pan.

4.   Remove from the oven and let cool for a few minutes in the pan. Run a knife around the sides of the pan and slide the frittata onto a plate.

5.   Serve at room temperature, quartered or sliced into thin wedges, garnished with sour cream and caviar.

EGGS BENEDICT

This standard brunch dish packs a real surprise when you substitute smoked salmon for ham and top it all with salmon caviar. There are several elements that need coordination, but the final assembly takes only 5 or 6 minutes.

SERVES 4

Hollandaise Sauce

3 egg yolks
1 tablespoon lemon juice
6–8 ounces (1 1/2–2 sticks)
   unsalted butter

Salt
Freshly ground white pepper

---

8 large eggs
2 tablespoons white vinegar
4 English muffins, or 8 slices
   brioche or challah

2 tablespoons unsalted butter,
   at room temperature
1/2 pound smoked salmon,
   sliced
8 tablespoons salmon caviar

1.   Make the Hollandaise Sauce first because it is the element easiest to keep warm. I prefer to make the sauce in a bain marie fashioned with a small saucepan and large skillet, but you could also make it in a double boiler or directly over the heat in a heavy saucepan. Beat the egg yolks and lemon juice off the heat in a small, heavy saucepan or in the top of a double boiler until the yolks thicken.

2. Place the egg yolks and lemon juice in a larger pan of hot water (to come about 1 inch up the side of the saucepan) or in the double-boiler bottom over hot water, making sure the bottom of the pan doesn't touch the hot water. Beat constantly with a whisk, making sure all eggs are touched regularly by the whisk, until the eggs thicken considerably. If the water below cools, put it over low heat, but don't let the water boil and make sure you keep beating.

3. When the eggs are thick enough to coat a spoon heavily, start adding the butter, 1 teaspoon at a time. Fully incorporate each pat of butter before you add the next. When about half the butter is incorporated, you can add larger pats at once. When all the butter is incorporated, taste for seasoning. Add only a little salt and plenty of freshly ground white pepper, and more lemon juice if the sauce needs it. The sauce will keep warm for about 30 minutes in the bain marie filled with warm water. Heat, but don't come near the boil, if the water cools too much.

4. To poach the eggs, bring 7 cups water to a simmer in a skillet or round gratin pan about 2½ inches deep and 10 inches round. The water should be almost to the top of the pan. Add the white vinegar. At the same time, start toasting the bread.

The easiest way to poach eggs is to crack each one into a cup and then slip it gently into the water, which should never boil but be kept just beneath the simmer. With a tablespoon fold the strings of egg white that may spread over its yolk. Using the cup system, add each egg and poach for 4 minutes.

5. Remove the bread from the toaster or oven, and butter each piece. Put a generous slice of smoked salmon on top.

6. Remove each egg with a slotted spoon or flat skimmer and let all the water drain off. To remove any vinegar taste, plunge each egg into a bowl of warm water and let drain. Place 1 egg on each piece of bread, over the smoked salmon.

7. Put 2 tablespoons of the Hollandaise over each egg and top with 1 tablespoon of the caviar. Serve immediately.

SCRAMBLED EGGS WITH CAVIAR

Scrambled eggs should be creamy, soft curds that just hold their shape. They should be cooked over *very* low heat and stirred constantly. It's only a matter of three or four minutes and the attention required is worth it.

SERVES 4−5

8 *large eggs*	2 *tablespoons heavy cream*
Salt	8 *tablespoons caviar: beluga,*
Freshly ground black pepper	*sevruga, or domestic*
3 *tablespoons unsalted butter*	*sturgeon*

1.   Beat the eggs with a little salt and pepper for about 30 seconds.
2.   Heat the butter in a heavy cast-aluminum, stainless-steel, or enamel skillet, 7 to 8 inches in diameter.
3.   Pour in the eggs and, stirring constantly with a whisk or wooden spoon, cook over very low heat, reaching all over the bottom of the pan. Steady, fast whisking or stirring will ensure creamy eggs. After 2 or 3 minutes, the eggs will form a slightly granular custard. Keep breaking the curds; the smaller the curd, the creamier the eggs will be. The eggs should be soft, but set when you serve them. Remove from the heat when the eggs are just short of done. They will continue to cook in their own heat. Immediately stir in the heavy cream and then the caviar. Turn out onto a platter and serve at once.

NOTE: Michel Guérard serves scrambled eggs in their shells with caviar, as an elegant first course. Carefully cut the raw eggs with a serrated knife about ½ inch down from the point end. Empty the eggs into a bowl. Wash the shells carefully in warm water and turn upside down on paper towels to dry. When the eggs are done, put each empty shell in an egg cup and fill ¾ full with the scrambled eggs. Top with 1 tablespoon caviar, slightly domed. Put the top on and serve with toast or warm cooked asparagus to be dipped into the egg and caviar.

CAVIAR OMELETTE

An omelette takes some practice to master, but once you do it's a cinch. Though a poor workman blames his tools, you really do need a good nonstick pan to make a proper omelette. For years, I have used a long-handled, seasoned iron pan, 7 inches in bottom diameter with 2-inch sloping sides. Teflon-coated aluminum or highly polished aluminum with those same dimensions are both fine.

The pan and the butter must be very hot, and you should remember that one omelette serves one person. It is far easier to make three or four omelettes in succession than to attempt to make one omelette for four people.

There is no spilling or shaking or flipping in the omelette technique I give here. It's not a performance, but it's a good omelette.

3 eggs
Salt
Freshly ground black pepper
1 teaspoon vegetable oil

1 ½ tablespoons unsalted
butter
½ cup sour cream
2 tablespoons salmon caviar

1.   Break the eggs into a small bowl, add a pinch of salt and a few grindings of black pepper. Combine with a fork just until the whites and yolks are mixed. Don't beat the eggs to a froth or you'll get a tough omelette.
2.   Heat the vegetable oil in the pan. This allows the pan to get very hot without burning the fat. Wipe the pan out with paper towels and add the butter.
3.   Immediately pour in the eggs. In 4 or 5 seconds, the eggs will set. Stir the center once or twice with the flat of a fork. With the tines of a fork, lift the edges and rotate the pan so the uncooked eggs from the center flow underneath and around the sides. In a minute the center will be soft and the underside lightly browned and set.
4.   Slide the omelette onto a plate and fill half with the sour cream and caviar. Fold over and serve.

EGG CAROLINE

Lydie Marshall, the great cooking teacher and author of *Cooking with Lydie Marshall*, gave me this recipe. She remembers eating this dish years ago at Jacques Manière's restaurant on the Boulevard St. Germain in Paris. This dish demonstrates the great affinity of fish eggs with hen's eggs.

SERVES 1

1 large egg
1 tablespoon crème fraîche (see page 31) or heavy cream

1 tablespoon imported or domestic sturgeon caviar

1.   Gently tap the egg on a counter to determine if it is cracked. A hollow sound means the egg is cracked and should not be used for this dish. Place the egg in a small saucepan and cover with cold water. Bring to a boil, lower the heat, and cook at a gentle boil for 2½ minutes (if you use extra large or jumbo eggs, cook for half a minute more). You want a very soft yolk and almost-firm white.

2.   Stand the egg in an egg cup and with a serrated knife, cut off the top. Gently spoon in the crème fraîche or cream and top with the caviar. Serve at once. If you don't have an egg cup, spoon the egg into a small ramekin and add the cream and caviar.

SALADS AND SANDWICHES

Some of these salads are excellent first courses or entrées, others are good as accompaniments to roasts, cold meats, and pâtés. The sandwiches are grand indulgences.

"There is an Italian sauce called *caviaro*, which begins to be in use with us, such vain affectors are we of novelties. It is prepared of the spawn of the sturgeon: the very name doth well express its nature, that it is good to beware of it."

Latin *cave* $=$ be careful

TOBIAS VENNER,
Via recta (1620)

CHICK PEA SALAD À LA MARTEGALE

Boutargue, the "Provençal caviar" made from dried, pressed gray mullet roe, is a specialty of Martigues, near Marseilles. *Botarga*, available in this country, is a close relative of *boutargue*. It is made from dried, pressed tuna roe and has a strong flavor. *Botarga* is wonderful in this chick pea salad. You can buy *botarga* either already grated or wrapped in beeswax to peel and grate yourself.

SERVES 4−6

1 pound dried chick peas, or one 19-ounce can chick peas
1 clove garlic
Salt
Freshly ground black pepper
½ teaspoon dry mustard
1 small onion, minced
2 tablespoons lemon juice
6 tablespoons olive oil

2 small green peppers, seeded and cut into julienne strips
2 tablespoons (½ ounce) grated botarga
Nutmeg
4 tablespoons chopped parsley
2 tablespoons chopped chives
Niçoise olives
Anchovy fillets

1.   If you are using dried beans, put them in a large pot with two or three times their volume of water. Bring to a boil, cover, remove from the heat, and let stand for 1 to 2 hours. Bring the beans and the soak water to a boil, cover, reduce heat to very low, and simmer the beans until they are tender but still hold their shape, anywhere from 1 to 2 hours. Drain the beans in a colander and pat dry between layers of paper towels.

If you are using canned beans, drain them of their liquid and place in a colander. Wash under cold running water until the water runs out clear. Pat the beans dry between several layers of paper towels. Wet beans will dilute the dressing and make the salad soggy.

2.   In the bowl in which you plan to serve, mash the garlic and combine it with a pinch of salt, pepper, dry mustard, onion, and

lemon juice. Slowly beat in the olive oil. Add the drained and dried chick peas and julienned green peppers. Grate or sprinkle over the *botarga* and a few gratings of nutmeg. Mix and let sit for at least 30 minutes, giving the beans time to absorb the dressing.

3.   Just before serving, toss in the parsley and chives and garnish the salad with olives and anchovies.

WHITE BEAN SALAD

This Italian salad used to be made of caviar from Po River sturgeon, which, alas, is no longer plentiful.

SERVES 4–6

1 pound dried white beans, or
    one 19-ounce can cannel-
    lini or other white beans
3 tablespoons olive oil
1 tablespoon lemon juice
4 tablespoons minced red
    onion

Salt
Freshly ground black pepper
4 tablespoons domestic
    sturgeon caviar

1.   Put the dried beans in a large pot (the beans will triple in volume during their cooking) with two or three times their volume of water. Bring to a boil, cover, remove from the heat, and let stand for 1 to 2 hours.

2.   Bring the beans and the soak water to a boil, cover, reduce heat to very low, and simmer the beans until tender but still firm, anywhere from 45 minutes to 1½ hours, depending on the size of the beans and their freshness. Drain the beans in a colander and pat dry between several layers of paper towels.

If you use canned beans, drain them of their liquid and then place in a colander. Wash under cold running water until water runs out clear. Pat the beans dry between several layers of paper towels. Wet beans will dilute the dressing and make the salad soggy.

3.   In the bowl in which you plan to serve, whisk together the olive oil, lemon juice, minced red onion, salt, and pepper. Add the beans and stir to combine. Set aside until ready to serve; a wait of an hour or so will give the beans time to absorb the dressing.

4.   Just before serving, gently stir in 3 tablespoons of the caviar; mound the final tablespoon in the center.

COMPOSED SALAD

This salad is beautiful to look at; even confirmed greens-haters have asked for seconds. The various elements should be prepared in advance; the final assembly takes just a minute or two. The quantities below will serve six as an appetizer and three or four as a main course.

½ pound salad greens, one
   alone or a combination:
   leaf lettuce, red-tipped
   lettuce, raddichio
2 tablespoons lemon juice
7 tablespoons olive oil
Salt
Freshly ground black pepper
1 teaspoon Dijon mustard
3 tablespoons minced shallots

3 tablespoons chopped parsley
12–14 red new potatoes
   (about ¾ pound)
1 small green pepper, seeded
   and cut into julienne strips
½ pound sliced smoked
   salmon
¼ cup sour cream or crème
   fraîche (see page 31)
4 tablespoons salmon caviar

1.   Tear the lettuce into manageable pieces; wash, dry, and refrigerate until ready to assemble the salad.

2.   In a medium-size bowl, combine the lemon juice, olive oil, salt, and pepper. Set aside 2½ tablespoons, and to the dressing remaining

in the bowl add the mustard, shallots, and 2½ tablespoons of the parsley.

3. Place the potatoes in a saucepan with cold water to cover and cook at a medium boil for 10 to 15 minutes, or until just tender.

4. Drain the potatoes, and while they are still warm, slice them into the bowl of dressing. Add the green pepper and toss gently to coat with the dressing. Let sit for 30 minutes at least, so the potatoes have a chance to absorb the dressing and the green pepper softens a bit.

5. Just before you are ready to serve, line a platter with the lettuce. Toss with the reserved 2½ tablespoons dressing. Place the potatoes and green peppers on top of the lettuce, scraping the bowl to get out all the dressing. Lay the smoked salmon on top of the potatoes and pat it with the sour cream or crème fraîche. Scatter the caviar over that and sprinkle with the remaining ½ tablespoon parsley.

TOMATOES WITH CAVIAR AND CRÈME FRAÎCHE

Really tasty tomatoes, ripe and juicy, make all the difference in this salad.

SERVES 6

3 ripe tomatoes	3 tablespoons minced shallots
Salt	or scallions
2 bunches arugula	2 tablespoons minced chervil,
3 tablespoons olive oil	chives, or parsley
1 cup crème fraîche (see page	3 tablespoons salmon caviar
31) or sour cream	

1. To peel the tomatoes, plunge them into boiling water for 10 seconds. Skin, and halve each one horizontally. Remove the seeds with the handle end of a spoon or with your thumb, and salt each

half lightly. Turn cut side down on paper towels and leave for 30 minutes.

2. Wash, stem, and dry the arugula. Arrange on a platter.

3. Just before serving, place the tomato halves on the greens and dribble each half with some olive oil.

4. Combine the crème fraîche or sour cream with the shallots or scallions and one or more of the minced herbs.

5. Put some crème fraîche on each tomato half and top each half with ½ tablespoon of the caviar.

FISH SALAD

This is a good way to use up leftover poached or steamed fish.

SERVES 3 – 4

1 pound cold poached sole or other firm, white-fleshed fish

8 tablespoons minced shallots or scallions

1½ tablespoons mayonnaise

1 tablespoon crème fraîche (see page 31) or sour cream

1 teaspoon lemon juice

2 bunches watercress

4 tablespoons golden white-fish caviar or salmon caviar

1. Coarsely chop the fish and place it in a bowl with the shallots, mayonnaise, crème fraîche or sour cream, and lemon juice. Mash with a fork.

2. Line a platter with the washed and dried watercress and place the fish salad on top. Spread the caviar over the fish salad and serve.

CHICKEN SALAD

This is a delicious and elegant dish for lunch, or a late supper when you don't want any last-minute fussing.

SERVES 5–6

4 cups diced cooked chicken
3 tablespoons lemon juice
4 tablespoons minced shallots
  or scallions
Freshly ground black pepper
3 tablespoons mayonnaise
1 tablespoon crème fraîche
  (see page 31) or sour cream

6 tablespoons salmon caviar
2 bunches watercress or
  arugula
3 tablespoons olive oil
2 ripe tomatoes, quartered

1. Moisten the chicken with 2 tablespoons of the lemon juice. Add the shallots or scallions and a generous amount of freshly ground black pepper. Let sit for 15 minutes, or longer.
2. Combine the mayonnaise and the crème fraîche. Stir in the chicken and then, gently, 3 tablespoons of the caviar.
3. Just before serving, put the greens on a platter and toss with the remaining tablespoon lemon juice and the olive oil. Mound the chicken salad on the greens and surround with tomato wedges. Place the remaining caviar in the center of the salad.

POTATO SALAD WITH CAVIAR

This salad is best served at room temperature, within an hour of making it. Don't throw away any leftovers, but do bring the salad to room temperature before serving again.

SERVES 5 – 6

2 pounds all-purpose potatoes
¼ cup mayonnaise
¼ cup sour cream
4 tablespoons minced scallions, including an inch or 2 of green top

1 tablespoon white vinegar
Freshly ground black pepper
Salt
4 tablespoons domestic sturgeon caviar

1.   In a saucepan, cover the potatoes with cold water, bring to the boil, and simmer until the potatoes are done—still firm but not hard. Cooking times vary according to the size and type of potato.
2.   Combine the mayonnaise, sour cream, scallions, and white vinegar in the bowl in which you plan to serve the salad.
3.   While they are still warm, peel the potatoes and slice about ½ inch thick directly into the dressing. Add a generous amount of freshly ground black pepper and just a little salt.
4.   Just before serving, gently stir in the caviar, reserving a teaspoon to mound in the center.

POTATO SALAD WITH PRESSED CAVIAR

This salad is made with pressed caviar. It is served as a first course, without any other food to distract you from it.

SERVES 4

4 tablespoons pressed caviar
½ cup crème fraîche (see
  page 31)
¼ cup heavy cream

2 tablespoons lemon juice
Freshly ground black pepper
16 small red-skinned potatoes
  (about 2 pounds)
Bibb lettuce

1.   With the back of a fork, mash the caviar and slowly whisk in the creams. Add the lemon juice and freshly ground black pepper. Let stand for 1 hour.

2.   Put the potatoes in a saucepan with cold water to cover, bring to a boil, and cook at a moderate boil until the potatoes are just tender, 10 to 15 minutes.

3.   Drain the potatoes and when cool enough to handle, slice them ¼ inch thick directly into the dressing. Toss gently.

4.   Put the lettuce leaves on a platter, or on individual plates, and top with the salad.

RUSSIAN SALAD

This composed vegetable salad is dressed with what is perhaps a fantasy of the original Russian dressing: Craig Claiborne believes it was made with mayonnaise, beets, and caviar. Whether authentic or not, it's mighty good.

SERVES 10–12

1 pound green beans
3/4 pound turnips or rutabaga
1 1/2 pounds new potatoes
3/4 pound carrots
3/4 pound shelled peas, fresh or frozen

3/4 pound frozen lima beans
Lettuce leaves
1/2 cup minced scallions, including green tops

Russian Dressing

2 egg yolks, at room temperature
1 egg, at room temperature
1 teaspoon Dijon mustard
3 tablespoons lemon juice
3/4 cup olive oil
1/2 cup vegetable oil

Freshly ground black pepper
Salt
8 tablespoons minced or grated cooked beets
8 tablespoons caviar: imported or domestic sturgeon, golden whitefish, or salmon

1. String and trim the green beans to about 1 1/2 inches. Peel and coarsely dice the turnip. Scrub the potatoes and quarter them. Scrape the carrots and cut into julienne strips.
2. Bring a large quantity of *unsalted* water to a boil. Cook the green beans for 1 minute, salting them when the water returns to the boil. This will set their color. Drain in a colander and plunge into a bowl of ice water. Dry on paper towels. Repeat for the other fresh vegetables, starting each time with fresh cold water. The turnips will take about 5 minutes; the potatoes, 10 to 15; the peas, 30 seconds if frozen, 2 minutes if fresh; the carrots, about 5 minutes; and the

limas, about 10 minutes. The vegetables should retain their crunchy texture. Combine the towel-dried vegetables in a large bowl.

3. To make the dressing, put the yolks and whole egg, along with the mustard and lemon juice, into the container of a blender or food processor. Run the machine for 20 seconds. With the motor running, add the oils in a thin, slow stream. Remove the mayonnaise to a small bowl and taste for seasoning: it may need more lemon juice. Add freshly ground black pepper and a little salt to taste. Then add the beets.

4. Just before serving, line a platter with washed and dried lettuce leaves. Add 6 tablespoons of the caviar to the mayonnaise and gently combine with the vegetables. Pile the salad on the lettuce leaves and sprinkle the top with the scallions. Garnish the salad with the remaining caviar.

NOTE: The mayonnaise will keep refrigerated for several days but should be brought to room temperature before mixing with the vegetables. The vegetables should be served the day they are cooked.

TURKEY SANDWICH

This is as good a turkey sandwich as you are ever likely to eat.

SERVES 1

¼ pound turkey, sliced off the bird
Two ½-inch-thick slices black bread

2 tablespoons Russian Dressing (see page 141)

1. For the best turkey sandwich ever, the meat should be sliced off a perfectly cooked, juicy bird who saw service hot no more than a day or two before you make the sandwich.

2. Slather each piece of bread with Russian Dressing. Lay the turkey on one slice and cover with the other.

Variation: You can substitute very good fresh bakery white bread or a French baguette, if you slice it horizontally. Make sure the bread is not sweet.

SMOKED STURGEON AND CAVIAR SANDWICH

This is a wonderful sandwich to eat if you have a little leftover caviar, not enough to share, but plenty for one. This is an open-face sandwich, best eaten with your fingers.

SERVES 1

*Two ¼-inch-thick slices black
  bread or very fresh bakery
  white bread
1 tablespoon unsalted butter
¼ pound smoked sturgeon
Lemon juice*

*Freshly ground black pepper
2 tablespoons (or more)
  caviar: beluga, osetra, or
  sevruga
Parsley sprigs*

1. Butter the bread and lay the smoked sturgeon on top. Sprinkle with lemon juice and freshly ground black pepper. Smooth the caviar on top and garnish with parsley.

Variation: Substitute smoked salmon and salmon caviar for the sturgeon and black caviar. Some people might want to substitute cream cheese for the butter.

" 'The trouble always is,' [James Bond] explained to Vesper,
'not how to get enough caviar, but how to get enough toast
with it.' "

IAN FLEMING,
Casino Royale

Index